Signed,
Sealed,
Delivered

Center Point
Large Print

Also by Nina Sankovitch and available from
Center Point Large Print:

Tolstoy and the Purple Chair

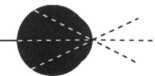

**This Large Print Book carries the
Seal of Approval of N.A.V.H.**

Signed, Sealed, Delivered

Celebrating the Joys
of Letter Writing

Nina Sankovitch

CENTER POINT LARGE PRINT
THORNDIKE, MAINE

This Center Point Large Print edition
is published in the year 2014 by arrangement with
Simon & Schuster, Inc.

The text of this Large Print edition is unabridged.
In other aspects, this book may vary
from the original edition.
Printed in the United States of America
on permanent paper.
Set in 16-point Times New Roman type.

ISBN: 978-1-62899-123-9

Library of Congress Cataloging-in-Publication Data

Sankovitch, Nina.
  Signed, sealed, delivered: celebrating the joys of letter writing / Nina
Sankovitch. — Center Point Large Print edition.
  pages ; cm
  Summary: "Sankovitch goes on a quest through the history of letters to
discover and celebrate what is special about the handwritten letter,
examining not only historical letters but also the letters in epistolary
novels, her husband's love letters, and dozens more sources. Sankovitch
reminds us that the letters we write are as important as the ones we wait
for"—Provided by publisher.
  ISBN 978-1-62899-123-9 (library binding : alk. paper)
  1. Letter writing—Social aspects.
    2. Written communication—Social aspects.
    3. English letters—History and criticism.
    4. English language—Rhetoric. 5. Letter writing—History.
    6. Letters in literature. 7. Large type books. I. Title.
PE1483.S217 2014b
809.6—dc23
                                                    2014007832

In memory of Robert F. Menz

Thou ugly, filthy, camel's face, You chid me once for not writing to you; now I have my revenge, and more justly chide you, for not having heard from you for so long as I fear you have forgotten how to write.

Elizabeth, Queen of Bohemia,
in a letter to the Earl of Carlisle, 1630

Table of Contents

Signed,
Sealed,
Delivered

Prologue

Thank you—that is for being born and for
the letters too.
—Letter from Georgia O'Keeffe
to Alfred Stieglitz

When my oldest son was still an only child,
my husband and I bought him his first chair
and desk. The three of us had set out for the
Chelsea flea market early one October morning.
The market was known for its collection of used
furniture, slightly bent lamps, and bizarre bric-a-
brac. We had no clear goal in mind other than
wandering through the outdoor aisles before the
popular spot became too crowded for a large-
wheeled stroller.

It was a day of big blue skies and fresh air after
a night of cleansing rain. We had nothing more
pressing to do than keep our thirteen-month-
old son happy. Full of young-parent energy and
caffeine, we walked the sixty blocks downtown.
Jack and I took turns pushing the stroller while
Peter entertained us with a constant barrage of
songs and chatter.

I don't remember who first spotted the small desk and chair, perfectly matched in slivered oak and inlaid scarring, bearing witness to at least one generation of scribblers before us. But there was no question in any of our minds: Peter thumped the desk with his fist and the set was ours.

We shoved the stroller, desk, and chair into the back of a large yellow cab and went home to the Upper West Side. I cleared out a corner of the living room for Peter's desk, just below a window and to the side of our nonworking but fine-looking fireplace. From our small kitchen alcove I would be able to keep an eye on the desk, and when I sat to read on the couch facing the fireplace, Peter would be there beside me, working away while I turned pages.

I set up jars of markers and crayons along Peter's desk, just where it met the brick wall. I laid out stacks of notebook paper, small index cards, and used envelopes, leaving the middle space of the desk open and clear. Above the jars I attached Peter's favorite postcard to the rough bricks, a portrait of Shakespeare: the writer looks grim, his lips set in a downward line between goatee and mustache. Five ounces of blue sticky gum held the card straight. Everything was set and ready.

Peter toddled on sturdy legs over to his desk, pulled out his chair, and began to scribble. He quickly covered an index card with blue marker squiggles, then carefully worked the card into an envelope. His face serious, he turned and handed me the envelope. I had received my first letter from Peter.

Flash-forward seventeen years, and it is another beautiful fall morning. Peter's old desk now sits in a sunroom off the main drag of the suburban home we moved to when our fourth child was born. Peter is away at college. We dropped him off there in August, moving him into his dorm on his eighteenth birthday. After getting him settled, we went out for lunch, to celebrate the birthday and the start of college.

"After we eat, you guys should get going," Peter said to me as we sat down in the French restaurant a block away from Harvard Yard.

"No problem." I nodded. I understood. He wasn't saying "hit the road" to me, not really. He was just saying that it was time for him to go his own way, and that family was not invited.

Within hours of leaving him on the steps of Memorial Hall, I got a text on my phone: "Love you."

I showed it to Jack.

"Nice," he said, and I agreed. Very nice.

But I wanted more. I wanted more than the texts and tweets and the occasional phone calls I got over the next few weeks. I wanted a letter.

"Drop me a line sometime," goes the old

farewell. A casual request, but for me a strong desire. With one child off at college, and three more to go, joining their brother in places near or far but *not* home with me, I wondered: Why does a letter mean so much?

1

Letters Found

Yet write, oh write me all, that I may join
Griefs to thy griefs, and echo sighs to
  thine.
  —Alexander Pope, *"Eloisa to Abelard"*

Y ears ago I found a trove of old letters. I
found them in a broken-down steamer trunk
buried under moldy blankets in a dilapidated shed
attached to a decrepit row house. The house was
on West Seventy-Eighth Street in New York City
and we'd just become its owner.

Jack and I had first heard about the old house
for sale in our neighborhood two months earlier.
On a cold November morning we took a walk over
to look at it. The windows of the redbrick town
house had a few cracked panes of glass and the
bricks needed a good cleaning, but otherwise the
place seemed solid. It was narrow, less than
seventeen feet wide, but a whopping five stories
tall. At the very top, a small, oblong window
blinked under a sharply curving roofline. The
house was charming and vaguely Amsterdamish

in the pitch of its roof, the rhythm of its rows of windows, and the arch of its front door.

Suddenly the front door was flung open. A well-dressed woman came out, pulling an old chair behind her. We watched as she struggled with the chair, trying to prop the door wide open.

Jack hiked up the stairs to help the woman with the door. Mission accomplished, he introduced us as interested buyers. The woman hesitated for a moment.

"The open house starts at one," she said, "and I just came by to clean up what I can . . . but if you'd like to come in, please do."

We followed her into a large hallway with stained but sturdy parquet floors and a winding staircase upholstered in worn red velvety carpeting. An octagonal lamp hung overhead, unlit.

"I thought the electricity was on, but I guess not," the real estate broker said. "Watch your step." She led us through the house, first going up the stairs to the very top floor. From there we saw that the house had only half a roof, the layers of old terra-cotta tiles broken and uneven, the plaster gone. Cold seeped in.

"No real functioning heating system," we were told. "The boiler hasn't worked in years."

It quickly became apparent that the plumbing also had failed in times long gone by. When Jack turned on the faucet in a bathroom painted lime green, the walls of the dark purple bedroom next door spouted mini-fountains of water. The pipes had been frozen and burst so many times, leaks ran in lines across the cracked walls.

The broker shrugged and led us downstairs, all the way down to the ground floor. As she walked back to show us the overgrown garden, she suddenly pitched forward. Jack grabbed her just in time, holding her tightly and pulling her up and out of a large opening in the spongy floor.

"Better get upstairs," he said, and she agreed.

We sat in the front hallway, the three of us perched on broken and dusty chairs, and she told us a bit of the history of the house. It had been owned by the same family for over a century but the family was long gone.

"No one has lived here in over fifteen years," she explained.

"We love it," I burst out, and Jack nodded in agreement.

Who couldn't love this house, even if it was unlit, unroofed, unheated, unplumbed, and with rotting floors? Built in 1888, it still had the original stained glass in the front windows and an ornate rounded staircase leading upward under a lead-paneled glass skylight. The ceilings on every floor were high, the moldings along the walls exquisite, and every room had a fireplace, with borders and mantels made of thick marble and elaborately tiered wood. Each fireplace was different from the other. One was so elaborately tiered, there would be a place for every framed family photo we owned. We belonged in this house.

Our offer for the house was accepted. More and more offers kept coming in, higher and higher, but the seller remained firm. Our own lawyer couldn't believe it.

"The family won't back out on the deal," he told us. "They have a good feeling about you." Real estate in New York City sold on good karma: unheard of.

And then more good karma: we found Joseph, a contractor willing to work with us to put our house back into working order for a price we could afford. It was Joseph who first discovered the trunk of letters. A few days after we closed on the property, he called me on my cell phone. He'd begun cleaning the place out, bringing in a crew of strong young men to work.

"Come over, we found something in the back-yard."

When I arrived at the house, Joseph gestured to me to follow him downstairs. We passed through the lower floor, the boards now reinforced and solid, and out the back door. The yard behind our house was small and had been used for years by the neighbors as a dump site. One green bush flourished in a corner but the rest was littered with trash, covering the weeds struggling to get through. Joseph led me over to a shed attached to our house at one corner.

The small shed was made of plywood and covered with a corrugated tin roof. A torn screen acted as the door. I entered the small, dark space and waited for my eyes to adjust.

Taking up most of the space was a steamer trunk. It was an old-fashioned one made of panels of wood with bands of steel across the middle. The trunk had sunk into the dirt floor. I could see that the bottom section had rotted out, leaving the bands of steel flexing in vain.

I remember opening the trunk with a shiver of excitement. A cascade of bundled letters fell out, released from decades of interment. They were dusty and musty but surprisingly sturdy. The bundles had been tied up tightly in blue and red ribbons. I loosened one of the bundles to take a look. The envelopes encasing the letters were easy to read and were mostly addressed to Mrs. Dewitt J. Seligman, or Mrs. Addie Bernheimer Seligman, or to Mr. and Mrs. Dewitt J. Seligman. I had found the letters collected and kept by Addie Bernheimer Seligman. Who was she? And how did this trunk come to be in this shed attached to my new house?

Below the packets and packets of letters were two cardboard boxes labeled "Cramer's Photo Dry Plates"; a flower-patterned box containing a ribbon-trimmed straw bonnet; a thick book bound in navy blue entitled *Who's Who in New York City* and published in 1918; and numerous bundles of tiny cardboard notices, wrapped in fraying twine. I pulled a notice out from one of the bundles. It was a reply card for a wedding:

Mr. and Mrs. Julius Kohn will attend.

Further digging revealed a yellowed *New York Times* newspaper, slid in among the bundles of replies. It had been folded back to the society announcements. In between the notices of the wedding of Miss Eugenia, daughter of N. A. Jennings, to Lieutenant Daniel H. Kingman (as noted in the piece, "the two older sisters of the bride had already found husbands in the army") and the charitable gift of Mrs. John Jacob Astor ($1,500 to the Children's Aid Society to fund the permanent housing "in the West for 100 destitute boys of New York"), I read the announcement for the wedding between Addie Bernheimer and Dewitt Seligman, celebrated the day before, on June 5, 1878. The ceremony and the reception were held at the house of the bride's family on West Fourteenth Street:

Both families are well known in social and business circles, the Bernheimers being wealthy real-estate owners and the Seligmans being of the firm of J. & W. Seligman & Co. . . . Both families are very large, and their members alone numbered some two hundred persons . . . the presents numerous and costly . . . At the reception, nearly five hundred people were present.

I lifted the blue Crane's boxes out of the trunk. Inside I found glass plate photographs of the couple's honeymoon at Niagara Falls. One photo had been printed and placed into a gilded frame. In the photo, the pair of newlyweds face each other on the cliffs just above the falls. Addie sits stiffly in a chair with Dewitt beside her in another chair, his mustache curled to perfection and the swell of his sideburns matching the swells of the falls behind. A bonnet perches on the top of Addie's upswept hair. I was suddenly sure I had seen that hat before. Back to the trunk to find the flower-patterned box. I opened the box and there it was: the hat Addie Bernheimer Seligman wore on her honeymoon, over one hundred and thirty years ago, perfectly preserved.

"I've got to get this stuff back to the family," I told Joseph.

I drove over to Home Depot in Queens to pick up plastic bins for the contents of the old trunk, and then spent the rest of the day loading them up. I packed in bundle after bundle of letters, and packet after packet of wedding reply cards, and brought the bins back to our apartment.

The next morning I called our real estate lawyer.

I described what I had found in the old shed. A few days later, he called me back. The sellers didn't want the trunk or any of the stuff I'd rescued from its rotting shell.

"They want you to have the letters. It's part of the sale, it all goes to you."

I hung up the phone and wandered down our long hallway, the only place where I'd found room for the plastic bins. I opened one up, the same shiver of excitement that I'd felt a few days before coursing through me. But now I was the undisputed heir to the found bounty.

It was late winter when I discovered the trunk full of Addie Seligman's letters and almost winter again before I had read through them all. I had a part-time job back then, three little kids, one teenage stepdaughter, a house renovation to oversee, and little time to read through stacks of letters wholly unrelated to my family or me. But whenever I had a free moment, I returned to the letters. They fascinated me and drew me into a world long gone.

Dewitt's letters to his wife were written in an elegant hand but difficult to decipher, penned from metal nibs dipped in ink. One of the first letters I could puzzle out was so funny that I laughed aloud when reading it. It was a letter Dewitt wrote to Addie, dated "April 29, '79." I had to remind myself it was 1879, just fourteen years after the Civil War had ended. Rutherford B.

Hayes was president, Gilbert and Sullivan were writing their operettas, Thomas Edison was working out the glitches of an electric light, and Dickens had died just nine years earlier.

But none of that figured into Dewitt's letter of advice to his beloved wife, written to celebrate the "b-a-b-y" that was due to arrive very soon; he described the soon-to-be-born child as "a little bit of a thing, which you can put in your pocket or stick up your nose for shelter when it rains." His advice begins with the importance of keeping "its toes scrupulously clean." He goes on to say that Addie as mother must "forbid" her child "from eating pate de foie gras the first three days of its life." By the sixth day, Dewitt counsels, the child will be ready for "baseball on the open lot," and by the tenth day, "let it run for Congress."

I could not decipher the final line: it was either "Your son will then be a marvel" or "Your son will then be a novel." But in fact, that much-anticipated son was never to be. When I went to search for the birth, I could find none recorded. I cried, as the young couple must have as well. First anticipation and laughter, then loss and tears. In 1880, a daughter, Ethel, was born. Two more children followed, Alma in 1883, and James in 1890.

Ethel was my link to the letters. In the early 1900s, Ethel wed Dr. Edgar Dinkelspiel and moved into his house on West Seventy-Eighth

25

Street. She raised two boys there, Edgar and Gerald. Her elder, Edgar, went on to become commissioner of Long Branch, New Jersey, and a man about town, while her younger, Gerald, stayed on in the house on West Seventy-Eighth until the end of his life, trading postage stamps by mail and staying out of the public eye. His grandmother Addie must have left the trunk with her daughter Ethel. Ethel left it with Gerald, and Gerald put it in the shed out back in the yard.

I could find only one letter from Ethel in the trunk, a sad missive of sorrow following the 1921 death of "my best friend, my husband." I also found one letter from the younger sister, Alma, undated, in which she complained about the persistence of a suitor to whom she was "giving the cold shoulder, alas in vain." The overwhelming majority of the letters that Addie kept and collected were the letters written by her only son, James Bernheimer Seligman. I found hundreds of letters in the trunk from James, dating from his childhood through the end of Addie's life in 1937. Most of the letters were written during his years at Princeton, from 1908 through 1912.

James's letters hooked me from the first looping words of greeting: "Dearest Mamma" or "Darling Parents." And the final sign-off—almost every note and letter ended with "your loving son James"—sealed the deal. I fell in love with a man who had lived a century before me.

• • •

The Seligman family came to the United States from Germany in the early 1800s. They began as peddlers and shop owners. As they prospered, they moved into banking and manufacturing. During the Civil War, the Seligmans supplied the Union uniforms and funding by securing foreign bonds. Two towns and one railroad locomotive were named for the Seligman family and in the old *Who's Who in New York City* I found row upon row of their names.

In 1894, when mining heir Benjamin Guggenheim secured James's aunt Florette in marriage, it was viewed as a coup for the up-and-coming Guggenheims to be associated with the older, established Seligmans. The Seligmans barely approved, sending a telegram to their European cousins: "Florette engaged Guggenheim smelter." Peggy Guggenheim, offspring of the marriage, writes in her autobiography that the cousins misinterpreted it as "Florette engaged. Guggenheim smelt her."

Perhaps the Seligmans softened when Ben Guggenheim went down on the *Titanic*, dressed with his steward for the occasion in dinner jackets and famously stating: "We've dressed up in our best and are prepared to go down like gentlemen."

Dewitt Seligman, brother of Florette, husband of Addie, and father of James, received a law degree from Columbia but never practiced, instead acting as a stockbroker with a seat on the exchange and as a banker with J. & W. Seligman. He also wrote plays (nearly every play ended with an explosion of some kind and not a single play was ever produced); served on the New York City Board of Education; published and edited a magazine called *Epoch*; and served for decades as a trustee of the Association for Improving the Condition of the Poor.

Addie's family, also German Jews who had come to the United States early in the nineteenth century, was rich in real estate and socially acceptable to the Seligman family (in contrast to her sister-in-law's choice of Benjamin Guggenheim).

But I didn't fall for James because of his pedigree or his money or his connections. I fell for his letters. From the sweet early notes in which he practices his handwriting ("Dear Mamma, Do you think my writing has improved any?") to the letters he wrote while off at college, and the notes he dashed off later while working and traveling, James was a sweet and funny and affectionate correspondent.

He wrote home almost daily, and sometimes twice or three times a day, during his years at Princeton. Woodrow Wilson was president of the university at the time and in the middle of his fight to close what he called "the elitist" eating clubs. James would take all his meals in "the commons" dining hall as a freshman and sophomore, but he didn't mind. In fact, James seemed to love everything about Princeton: "This is a bully place and I am enjoying it immensely," he wrote during his first fall there.

Whether scrawled quickly or with the words languorously rounded out, James's letters home from college are portraits of a young man with a history of delicate health but possessed of a robust appetite for experience, pleasure, and fun: "I am getting a good college education, developing like a film, apologizing to the grass every time I step on it, scrambling like an egg, yelling like a bear, telling the upperclassmen to go to @#$."

Studying didn't seem to interest him too much: "I will study later after my nap," and fun was to be had in many places: "I saw the game with Penn last night (basketball). It was interesting. The game? Oh no. The girl I was sitting next to . . ." Even the freshman hazing by upperclassmen made him laugh: "They asked me for my freshman cap . . . I haven't the slightest idea what they wanted it for, except to pretend they were freshys too. Anyhow, I handed it to them, and gave them my address, so I could get it back. I haven't much hopes however." Then, in an added postscript, "Hurrah! I just got my hat back! The hazing has begun and it is a lot of fun."

A typical college student, he always seemed to be in need of money: "As I have to pay $1.35 a day for meals until college opens [he'd arrived early], my supply of cash is almost extinct. I haven't opened a bank account, as you advised me not to, so that's how the math stands. The latest is black garters, so blew myself to a pair." (Hint, hint. Send more money.) And money was sent: "I cashed your first check, and found very little trouble in cashing it. In fact, if you have any more checks you need cashed, kindly forward same, and I will oblige."

Four years of college later, he is still happy for the checks: "Your letter and your check couldn't have possibly been more welcome—especially the latter. If you send a check with every letter, write as often as you want, twice a day if necessary."

His sweet nature comes through in the self-deprecating jokes ("I am once more sorry to say, with tears in my nose, and with shaking toes, etc that I didn't pass French . . . Thanking you again for your kind applause, I will close as Le Student Francais"); the small details about his day ("Chapel was great. I never laughed so much in my life"); and in answering what he called the "ponderous interrogations" sent by his mother: "My diet consists principally of food. My health is fine."

James writes of his classes—"Woodrow Wilson lectures to us in Jurisprudence—It is a treat to listen to him speak"—and of his newfound passions, including a love of Dickens: "I finished

Bleak House, and enjoyed the last 100 pages more than anything I have ever read in my life—Am going to get Oliver Twist tonight."

Some of his letters are short, as was his very first from Princeton, written the day he arrived on September 22, 1908: "Arrived safely. No headache. Have posted this as soon as I got off train. Will write soon." But most of the letters James wrote home are much longer, especially those in which he reassures his mother as to his health. He was a sickly teenager (a letter from the headmaster at Columbia Grammar School advised against sending James to Harvard in 1906: "Attend to the rest and development of his slender body and give him that healthy physical foundation on which success largely and happiness mainly depend"—the parents waited two years and sent James to Princeton) and James is constantly assuring his mother, "I am feeling fine."

In one letter, James describes having his nose cauterized against colds ("Breathe with your mouth closed, James," he admonishes himself) and tells his mother his surefire method of fighting off sore throats: with warm drinks and a soft pillow.

Despite his best efforts, in 1911 James contracted scarlet fever after attending a dance in New York City. He was in quarantine for seven weeks, held in "a private sanitarium" in "a magnificent four-story brownstone mansion at number 35 West Seventy-Second street," according to an old *New York Times* clipping I found among the letters. The house belonged to his aunt Belle and he was quarantined there along with two cousins, a Bernheimer and a Guggenheim.

When James was finally released, he promptly wrote to his parents eight pages filled with anecdotes about his illness—"It was almost worthwhile being ill, everyone was so attentive—I think everyone of my friends without exception sent me something or other, and Aunt Belle was much too kind"—and offered ample promises as to the state of his health: "I had a salt water bath this morning—simply great. You have no idea the way I feel—never felt half as strong in my life so please don't worry. I wish you could only see me, and then all your fears would be immediately dispelled."

He would write again and again promising his vigilance against further illness, as when he wrote: "My vaccination did not annoy me in the least at any time, and has now entirely healed." Then quickly changing the subject, he writes, "Irving's letters are interesting but I have had no time to read any of them yet. Please send me more."

Poor Irving, whoever he was, just didn't rate the read. James's letters, however, most certainly did, and I kept on reading and reading. Snatching fifteen minutes before starting dinner or tackling the laundry or heading off to work, I would sit beside the bins in my crowded hallway and read. Or late into the night, cat at my side, I sat on the hall floor and worked my way happily through a bundle or two of letters.

James continued to write to his mother after college, even when they were both living in New York City. Mail delivery was twice daily then and he wrote often, assuring his mother "I am feeling fine" and offering up jokes on an almost daily basis: "shall land on the N.Y.S. Ex. Sept.25th. Stocks will then drop 20 to 40 points according to which ones I buy."

He wrote to his mother when she traveled, going for the summer months to Loon Lake in the Adirondacks or to Lenox, Massachusetts, in the Berkshires; and when he traveled, writing from the wealthy resort town of Elberon on the Jersey Shore, where he spent many social weekends ("going to a dance as Esther's twin—will need a number of pillows for padding!") and from points around the world, including London ("the food is English, that is to say bad, but the atmosphere is lively"), Paris ("absolutely dead boring this time of year—we leave for Deauville in the morning"), Biarritz ("there are only two good hotels in Biarritz, the Carlton and Du Palais, and reservations will be found!"), Deauville ("yours truly won a golf tournament, because everyone else had gone off to goggle at the King of Spain"), Palermo ("such a view I have never seen"), and California ("I love everything out here—still, I love one or two things in N.Y.").

James cared little about current events, including politics. The presidential election of 1912, for example, was one of the most exciting in US history, with four parties battling it out. There was a split in the Republican Party between Theodore Roosevelt's progressive Bull Moose Party and the conservative followers of President William Howard Taft. James's old professor and Princeton president Woodrow Wilson ran for the Democrats, fighting hard for his place on the ticket. Eugene Debs ran for the Socialist Party. Roosevelt survived an assassination attempt but lost the election, Debs secured one million votes, the first and last time the Socialist Party would do so well in a presidential election, and Wilson won the presidency. But I could not find in any of James's letters a single mention of the election, nor any reference to having voted.

In 1920, James was eight years out of Princeton and working down on Wall Street. Exactly at noon on September 16, a horse-drawn buggy loaded with one hundred pounds of dynamite and five hundred pounds of cast-iron slugs drew up outside the J. P. Morgan bank and exploded. Thirty people were killed instantly, hundreds were injured, and windows up and down the street were blown out. The scene is described as one of horror:

The bomb . . . blew people apart where they walked out on a cool, late-summer day, tore arms and legs, hands and feet and scalps off living human beings. Others were beheaded or eviscerated, or found themselves suddenly engulfed in flames. Still more injuries were caused by a cascade of broken glass and the terrified stampede that followed.

James was working that day but all he had to say to his parents was a note quickly scribbled out and sent off: "Not hurt in explosion. Feeling fine." The blast was eventually attributed to anarchists and memorials were held for the victims, but James never mentioned the incident again. Perhaps he just did not like to write of glum or grim events: he shrugged off the April 1912 death of his uncle Benjamin on the *Titanic* by stating "I don't write condolences." Too bad, because with his capacity for gentle humor, he could have lifted the spirits of any survivor.

When I first read James's letters, my children were all under six years old. They were good kids, happy and active and curious. We were on the go all the time, with trips to the playground and to the library, hauling armloads of books upstairs to the children's room and back down again. Every day we needed to resupply ourselves with food and off we went to Fairway or Zabar's. I loaded our bags onto the stroller handles. If one of the children were to suddenly launch himself from the stroller, the whole thing would go off-kilter and bags would go flying.

My days were a haze of nonstop activity, some of it work, some of it play, with little time for things like long showers or long books or long *anything*. To steal a moment away with a letter from James Seligman was a treat. It was an escape from my life as a mother, a life I loved, into a life as a turn-of-the-century man about town, a life that fascinated me. I had a crush on the young man parading around the Princeton campus with such fun and flair. James was my handsome young boyfriend, although I have never seen a photo of him. It is only through his lovely handwriting and gift of words that I imagine him to be so handsome.

James provided me with a fantasy as I washed dishes and changed diapers and pushed strollers through Central Park. His letters allowed me, invited me, into his world. I was right there beside him as we went off on weekends to visit cousins on the Jersey Shore or met friends at the Century Country Club in Westchester—or better yet, on the Dinard golf course at Deauville on the west coast of France. Of course the details that James shared in his letters home were only part of the picture of his life; what young man shares all his experiences with his mother?

And so I filled in the rest, imagining evenings spent in New York, dancing and drinking gin; or long afternoons beachside in Biarritz, sharing cigarettes and champagne; or walking hand in hand across Cannon Green at Princeton in the crisp air of a fall afternoon, joining in the nattily dressed crowds expecting—and getting—a win in the 1911 football match against Harvard.

More than fourteen years have passed since I first read Addie's letters from her youngest child. I am no longer the young mother I was; I have one son in college and the other three are soon to follow. When I look over James's letters now, it is not with the warm rush of a young crush but with a softened maternal eye matched by an aching maternal heart. No longer filling in the blanks of what James left unsaid to his mother with fantasies of gin and late-night dancing, I shudder a bit at what my own son will leave unsaid in his letters home to me.

Rereading the letters of James Seligman proves all over again the power of the written, the hand-written, word. I fell in love with James Seligman, a young man who lived one hundred years ago, through his letters home. I remain loving toward him, as I might feel toward an old boyfriend. James has become a treasured friend and I care about him.

James is not a person I could have known without his letters. There is little other existing evidence of his life. I found a brief mention of him in a *New Yorker* article from 1954 titled "Sorting Out the Seligmans" and I found his name in an online family tree listing all the Seligmans of the nineteenth and twentieth centuries.

But I have James's letters and that's why he lives. Is that why his mother kept all those letters? So that some woman one hundred years in the future would know her son, love him, and, by remembering him, allow him to live on a bit longer? It would not have been a bad plan.

When Peter moved into his college dorm room, I left a present tucked into his bags of books and clothes: a box of ivory note cards with matching stamped envelopes.

2

Letters Saved

Sir, more than Kisses, letters mingle souls,
For thus, friends absent speak.
   —John Donne, *"To Sir Henry Wotton"*

The first letters I remember getting are the ones sent by my cousins in Belgium, slender blue sheets of paper that folded over to form airmail envelopes. Written in Flemish, they had to be translated by my mother. I loved the elegant notes even more for their indecipherable language, along with their strangely smoky smell and their stamps: a profile of their queen. I wrote back to my cousins in English, using our version of the thin blue airmail paper. It had red, white, and blue stripes along its folded edges and no queen in sight.

When I went away to camp in middle school, I wrote home for the first time, happy notes about horses and campouts under the stars, and seeing a calf born. I'd been awakened along with the other girls in my cabin by our counselor Marty in the middle of the night and led down under the light of a full moon to the cattle barn. There we watched as a wriggling, goop-covered, perfect little calf was pulled out of her manically lowing mom and placed gently onto the grass by Marty's farmhand boyfriend. The little calf lurched to her feet. She crowded in close to her mother, who seemed now to be almost purring.

I remember missing home then, acutely. Part of it was a reaction to seeing a mother and child discovering each other for the first time. But most of my homesickness came from wanting to share that moment of birth with my parents and my sisters, and yet I couldn't, because they were one hundred miles and one state away. By the time I wrote my letter to my parents, my wave of home-sickness had passed, but the poignancy of the event had not. I still had to share what I had seen.

In high school, I passed notes back and forth all day long at school, through any and all of my classes. Teenage hormonal imbalances released through the scribbling of a few sentences across a shred of paper, we commented on everything from Monsieur Lavering's new earring to John and Lisa's fifth breakup to plans for Friday night. A few of us even wrote notes after school and stuck them into envelopes for mailing. We'd shriek with laughter when a letter arrived a few days later: things changed fast in high school and a boy who had looked so cute on Monday was worth hardly a glance by Thursday and vice versa.

For years I kept a shoe box stuffed with those high school notes, but it disappeared during one of my moves. Now I save my letters in an old trunk. Not quite as big as Addie Seligman's trunk, my trunk is made of metal and wood. It is one of two used by my mother to move all of her possessions (and most of my father's) from Europe to the United States in the late 1950s.

When I was growing up in Illinois, my mother's trunks were kept in the basement of our house, set up on planks above the damp cement floor, their contents unknown to me. Only later did my sisters and I find out what was in the trunks: one held old photos, school notebooks, and letters, and the other, blankets that had been woven by my father's mother and sisters back in Belarus. My parents began to share the contents of the green trunks, handing out the blankets for us to keep and sharing the photos and letters, filling us up with stories circling the branches of our family tree.

When my parents moved out of the house I grew up in, my mother offered one of the old trunks to me, emptied now of its trove of blankets. I took the trunk and packed my own history into it, letters and notes and cards I'd received over the years. My trunk has become stuffed to the brim, holding everything from Jack's early postcards of love, to the RSVPs for my wedding (not quite as numerous or as elegant as those saved by Addie

Seligman), to my children's cards, concoctions of paste and glitter and scribbles, declarations of love from them to me. It is my green trunk of treasure.

Every year at Halloween I empty the trunk out, placing its contents in a corner of my room and covering the piles with a sheet. The trunk then serves as a coffin for our front hall, complete with glow-in-the-dark bones, severed limbs spattered with (fake) blood, and a few skulls lit up from inside by plug-in lights. When Halloween is over, the body parts are removed and the trunk once again becomes the place for my own letters.

Why do I hold on to all of these pieces of paper? For the same reason, I think, that Addie Seligman saved all of James's letters. Not for posterity. Addie knew what her son was like, and he was unlikely to make history, and while I do think my sons can change the world, those early homemade cards are not the proof of it. And while I do plan on leaving my letters behind when I've gone, I have no specific plans to leave them to this or that child; nor do I think Addie ever planned to share her collection with James himself one day. After all, the letters ended up with Ethel, not James, after Addie died.

I would guess that Addie saved her letters, like I do, to maintain a tangible, palpable bond between the past and the present, between the person she once was and the person she later became, and between a person she loved once and still did even after years passed by.

There have been times when I have needed reassurance that I am not floating out there alone in the universe, that I am tethered to people who will keep me secure. The letters offer that reassurance. Even if those people are gone, the bond endures through the tokens of connection we passed back and forth, the written manifestation of our relationship.

Six years before Peter left for college, my oldest sister, Anne-Marie, died of bile duct cancer. The cancer was brutal and fast, and she died within four months of her diagnosis. She had no time to say good-bye to her nephews—none of us realized how fast the end would be—and even my own last words to her were "See you tomorrow." Not that I would have wanted to say good-bye; what I wanted most desperately was to have hours and hours of conversation to store away and hold on to, to retrieve when I needed her, at that horrible time soon coming when she would no longer be with me.

I have a phone message from Anne-Marie on an old answering machine that I keep in a drawer and take out when I want to hear her voice. I have home movies of her, moments spent laughing with my boys, playing with them, and hamming things up for the camera. I also have photos galore, from our childhood together through her last trip to

India, taken just a month before she was diagnosed with cancer. And I have my memories of our conversations. I can remember all the summer nights we sat talking out on the front steps of our house when we were growing up, and the long evenings we spent together out on the roof of a building in New York City, accessed through a tiny window of an apartment she was subletting. I remember our conversations in her hospital room, me in a chair and Anne-Marie in the bed beside me.

But it is the written words she left me, postcards and birthday cards and letters exchanged over my forty-plus years of being her sister, that allow me to hold in my hand the very substance of who she was, to me and with me. To touch: I can hold my sister, still, in a very real and lovely and lasting way.

After Anne-Marie died, I searched through my green trunk and pulled out every bit of correspondence I'd saved from her. I found not only what she'd sent to me but what she'd sent to my four boys over the years, the birthday cards and postcards from all of her travels and sweet little notes she enclosed in the small gifts of books and toys that she gave to them.

For each of the boys, I want to create a box filled with the correspondence they received from Anne-Marie, along with photos of each of them with her. These boxes will allow each of my children to know, all over again, their aunt who loved each of them so very much. In feeling the same paper she felt, when she wrote to them years ago, and tracing her words with a finger, each boy can feel her embrace again.

When I touch the letters of James Seligman, I go back one hundred years. I am beside him as he bends over in his task of writing. I know him well, not only through touching the paper and the ink, or by reading what he wrote, but by deciphering his very person through the slant of his writing, the choice of paper, and the endearments he used.

I know it is imagination that allows me to see James's slender fingers forming the beautiful swirling *j*'s and *s*'s of his letters, to smell the lingering scent of his evening tobacco, and to feel his hand across mine. But the bond is not imagined: paper and ink have created a lasting connection between James and me.

The connection has made me a better person, if only for having laughed so much and indulged in so much pleasurable company through his letters. And isn't that what we say about our friends, that they have enriched our lives and made us better people? My friendship with James is one-sided, yes. But it exists nevertheless, and only exists because of what he wrote, so many years ago, in his efforts to relieve his mother's worries about him, and to amuse her. And so he has relieved and amused me. He has also made me more attuned to, and more appreciative of, the messages left for me in other letters.

I have a card on my desk, propped up on top of a stack of books, that my son George made for me when he was just five years old. Huge letters, in many colors and elaborately decorated with swirls and funny faces and waving hands, proclaim, loud and clear,

YOU KNOW WHAT? MOM upside down
is WOW!

George no longer thinks I am so "WOW" all the time. But his card tells me he once did, and that is good enough for me. Those words made me smile when I first saw the card, and they can make me smile all over again now, and in the future. In my green trunk, packed away just within reach, are more cards that can make me feel good; I am close to and loved by my children.

Letters are the history of our lives made solid, and they place us firmly within our history. Letters we save—the letters we *choose* to save—show us who we have embraced or surrounded ourselves with. They also show us who we have turned away from. I have letters from friends I no longer speak with and when I read what we once shared, I consider a move to reconnect. My best friend in high school, with whom so many scribbled notes were exchanged, has fallen off the map of my life, leaving only an address behind. I don't have her phone number and she ditched Facebook long ago. But I have an address for her, copied down from the last Christmas card she sent to me. The affinity between us is evidenced by our notes from our past and I am moved to repair the interrupted friendship by writing to her now, again.

Almost everyone I know has letters saved away somewhere, in shoe boxes or accordion-style file folders or in elegant gilded cardboard bought just for the purpose of holding and keeping letters. And when I ask people why they keep these letters, the answer is always the same. Because the letters are a link, a connection. My friends say things like "the writer is with me, to hold and cherish" or "I like seeing her hand-writing and remembering the time and place she was writing about" or "every time I reread these letters from loved ones, they appear in front of me, smiling, laughing."

When the letters we save are from people who are dead, whether it is for years or for centuries, we are preserving those people as a presence in our lives. We are allowing them to persevere as they once were: alive, vibrant, singular. One friend used her grandmother's letters to write a eulogy, presenting her vividly for everyone at the funeral service. Another friend describes the letters her mother left behind as a wonderful gift, keeping the bond between them alive.

My sister Anne-Marie was a fan of postcards, and she had a huge supply of them, picked up from museums and churches and villages all over Europe as she traveled around in pursuit of her research (she was a historian of Renaissance architecture).

The cards Anne-Marie sent still speak to me, not only in the image she chose to send (two crickets copulating to welcome me to college; joyous figures dancing to celebrate my passing of the bar exam; a Madonna and child after I gave birth to George) but, most important, in the words she scrawled in spidery letters across the back of each of them. Whether celebrating an event ("By the time you get this you'll be a real lawyer—congratulations") or expressing a known fact ("Paris is great—I don't know why we ever left") or admonishing me to keep a secret ("I was so exhausted I fainted outside of the theater—Don't tell Mama"), the physical reality of those cards and words and images means even more to me now than when I first got them in the mail. They are a tangible manifestation of our relationship as sisters and friends.

Letters provide not only a bridge back to the people from our past but also a bridge to those who are still very much in the present, but too far away for us to touch and see every day. Yes, I am getting texts from my son Peter off at college, short bursts of information and requests: "taking

Swedish, need honey" (and he really did mean "honey," not "money"—honey for his tea) and the treasured "love u." But these ten-character (or less) messages are not enough to salve how much I miss him.

A letter offers balm for the ache of missing Peter, because it is a physical connection. A letter gives me a feel for his mood not only in what he writes but also in *how* he writes. A letter, if I am lucky, offers the very smell of my child, his scent on the page, soap or sweat, confirming my knowledge of him as my son, always. A letter brings him home again.

3

Written Under the Cloak

I beg you to restore your presence to me
in the way you can—by writing me some
word of comfort.
> —*Letter from Heloise to Abelard*

In the middle years of the twelfth century, a
cloistered nun, abbess of her monastery in
northern France, wrote a letter to her lover,
recalling their past embraces: "Lewd visions of
pleasures take such a hold upon my unhappy soul
that my thoughts are upon their wantonness
instead of on prayers. . . . Youth and passion
and experience of pleasures which were so
delightful intensify my torments of the flesh and
longings of desire. . . ."

The woman was Heloise, and the man she loved
was Peter Abelard. The two met in the early 1100s
in Paris, where Abelard was a scholar and teacher
at the Cathedral of Notre Dame. He was the big
man on campus: "I began to think myself the only
philosopher in the world, with nothing to fear

from anyone." Students flocked to his lectures, friends gathered in the evening to hear him sing, and other scholars challenged him to debate, only to fail miserably against his fast-reasoning mind.

Heloise was living with her uncle Fulbert, filling out the education she'd begun in a convent by attending lectures and debates in Paris. Fulbert was known throughout the city as a canon of the Cathedral of Notre Dame. He was very proud of his niece and took her around with him, showing off her knowledge and charm.

It may have been during one of these outings that Abelard first noticed Heloise. He wrote to a friend, "In looks she did not rank lowest, whilst in the extent of her learning she stood supreme." In order to get closer to her, Abelard suggested to Uncle Fulbert that he become her tutor. Fulbert agreed and Abelard became a regular visitor to the home of Fulbert and Heloise.

Abelard and Heloise quickly discovered their mutual interests and attraction. Abelard wrote in a letter: "Need I say more? We were united, first under one roof, then in heart; and so with our lessons as a pretext we abandoned ourselves entirely to love . . . My hands strayed more often over the curves of her body than to the pages."

What a disaster when Uncle Fulbert discovered what had been going on in his house! He became enraged at what was happening under his nose, and adamant that punishment be exacted. Abelard blamed Heloise and begged Fulbert's forgiveness: "I protested that I had done nothing unusual in the eyes of anyone who had known the power of love, and recalled how since the beginning of the human race, women had brought the noblest men to ruin."

Abelard offered to marry Heloise but with a condition: their betrothal must remain a secret. To be a married man would undermine his credibility as both philosopher and religious teacher (the two professions were intertwined at the time). Fulbert agreed to the marriage and to the secret, but Heloise refused to go along with the plan. Even though she had become pregnant with Abelard's child, she preferred that both she and Abelard remain free to pursue their studies and their lives in their own way.

Abelard became frantic. He knew the damage Uncle Fulbert could wreak on his career; he wanted to appease the powerful man. He begged Heloise to marry him. Finally, she relented. Their child was born and they named him Astrolabe, after the couple's favorite navigational instrument. Abelard and Heloise were then married in a secret ceremony witnessed only by the priest and Uncle Fulbert. The baby was sent off to live with Abelard's sister. Heloise went to live once again with Fulbert. Abelard hoped that his life was finally back on track.

But Fulbert was vengeful. Shortly after the

wedding ceremony between his niece and her ex-tutor, Fulbert broke his promise of secrecy. He announced to the world that his niece was now the wife of Abelard and that the couple had a child. Abelard freaked out, hustled Heloise to a monastery outside of Paris, and holed up in his rooms at Notre Dame.

Furious that Heloise had been taken from him once again (perhaps the old uncle had a bit of a crush on her himself), Fulbert ordered his henchmen to attack Abelard. In the middle of the night, they entered his rooms by force and castrated the terrified scholar: "They cut off the parts of my body whereby I had committed the wrong of which they had complained."

Disgraced, Abelard went off to the Abbey of Saint-Denis while Heloise stayed on at her monastery at Argenteuil. They both officially entered their respective religious houses, Abelard with resignation ("Shame and confusion . . . brought me to seek shelter in a monastery cloister") and Heloise in "obedience with" her husband's wishes. Astrolabe stayed on with Abelard's sister. The family was separated, and even Fulbert was all alone.

The story of Abelard and Heloise seemed to have come to an end. But then in 1132 Abelard wrote a letter of consolation to a friend, explaining the whole sorry story of his relationship with Heloise. Letters of consolation are not like the condolence letters that we send today, written expressions of sympathy over the death of a loved one. In Abelard's time, letters of consolation were written to cheer up a depressed cohort. The idea was, *You think you've got it bad? Listen to how hard my life has been, and you'll feel better right away.*

Somehow Abelard managed to get a copy of his letter of consolation to Heloise. She was not pleased. She wrote to Abelard, chiding him for revealing "the pitiful story of our entry into religion and the cross of unending suffering." The happy ending he'd put to the story, furthermore, was not accurate: she was *not* happily reconciled to the religious life. "During the celebration of the Mass, when our prayers should be purer," she wrote to Abelard, "lewd visions of [our past] pleasures take such a hold of my unhappy soul that my thoughts are on their wantonness instead of on prayers."

Heloise implored Abelard, "You alone have the power to make me sad, to bring me happiness, or comfort. You alone have so great a debt to repay me, particularly now when I have carried out all your orders so implicitly that when I was powerless to oppose you in anything, I found strength at your command to destroy myself . . . God knows I never sought anything in you except yourself; I wanted simply you, nothing of yours. I looked for no marriage-bond, no marriage portion and it was not my own pleasures and wishes I sought to gratify, as you well know, but yours."

She asked that Abelard write to her and send some words of love and comfort; after all, she reasoned, "When in the past you sought me out for sinful pleasures your letters came to me thick and fast." She ended her plea with the simple salutation "Vale, unice." *Farewell, my only one.*

Abelard replied with a letter heavy with religious instruction. He ignored Heloise's plea for comfort and instead advised her to find solace in Christ. He demanded that she turn to prayer: "May divine mercy protect me through the support of your prayers and quickly crush Satan beneath our feet." He reminded her that as his wife she was "bound to do everything possible on my behalf . . . your chief concern must be the salvation of my soul."

Heloise had concerns beyond souls. Bodies still interested her, specifically his and hers. She admitted the pretense under which she operated daily—"Men call me chaste; they do not know what a hypocrite I am"—and wrote, freely and without restraint, about her sexual longings and religious misgivings, and about her undying love for Abelard.

How could Heloise write such letters, full of lust and love? Because she relied on the privacy of her communication. Under the cloak of discretion offered by the writing of a letter, Heloise could bare her soul. And she did, in letter after letter:

"My dear Husband . . . shall I never see you again? Shall I never have the pleasure of embracing you before death? What dost thou say, wretched Heloise? Dost thou know what thou desirest? Couldst thou behold those brilliant eyes without recalling the tender glances which have been so fatal to thee? Couldst thou see that majestic air of Abelard without being jealous of everyone who beholds so attractive a man? That mouth cannot be looked upon without desire; in short, no woman can view the person of Abelard without danger. Ask no more therefore to see Abelard; if the memory of him has caused thee so much trouble, Heloise, what would not his presence do? What desires will it not excite in thy soul? How will it be possible to keep thy reason at the sight of so lovable a man?"

The letters of Abelard and Heloise were hidden from prying eyes for almost one hundred years, the originals lost and copies locked away in Heloise's monastery. Finally discovered by someone digging around in the monastery's library, the letters began to make the rounds in late medieval Europe. Collected in a manuscript, the letters became hot stuff, the romantic scandal of the times, perfectly situated to illustrate the ideals of passionate love that were taking hold throughout Europe.

I found a Penguin translation of the letters in

a used bookstore in my hometown when I was fourteen years old. The bookstore was tucked away in an alley off the main street, heralded by a painted wooden sign hanging outside its door: no words, just the image of a stack of colorful books teetering against a black background. The narrow, winding store was dark and quiet, furnished with tattered velvet chairs, cobwebbed floor lamps, and shelves and tables overflowing with books.

Bookman's Alley was the final resting place for the book collections of some of the finest families of Chicago's North Shore. But those books, first editions and leather-bound volumes and barely cracked classics, were out of my price range. I could only afford the abandoned but once-beloved paperbacks left behind by passing-through Northwestern students.

The Letters of Abelard and Heloise. I had heard of the lovers. My mother was a medieval scholar and the Heloise story she shared with me and my two sisters over the dinner table was one in which a young woman disavows marriage in order to devote herself to studies. The Heloise she described to us, desexualized and intelligent, was glowingly presented as a certain kind of role model.

The Heloise I discovered that afternoon in Bookman's Alley, skimming through the pen-starred sections of the old paperback, was devoted to studying more than books. In underlined sentence after underlined sentence, she appeared to be interested, *very interested,* in sex. Together with Abelard, her older lover, "we lost all sense of shame and, indeed, shame diminished as we found more opportunities for love-making."

Shame? I blushed to the roots of my ponytailed hair. Love-making? This was hot stuff: "Pleasures which we shared . . . too sweet—they can never displease me, and can scarcely be banished from my thoughts. Wherever I turn, they are always there before my eyes, bringing with them awakened longings and fantasies which will not even let me sleep."

I closed the paperback with a jolt and stumbled to the front of the bookstore. A young man sat reading at the front desk. He ignored me as I stood before him, dollar bills in one hand and my chosen book in the other.

"I would like this, please," I said.

He looked up at me, then down at the book in my hand.

"The original star-crossed lovers," he murmured, and then looked up at me again. I felt as if I was being judged.

I must have passed muster, because he took my two dollars and waved me out of the store. I tucked the book under my coat and scooted away down the alley. Heloise and Abelard demanded the privacy of my room, and no dark corner in a bookstore would do.

I remember reading Abelard's lines, "Our desires left no stage of love-making untried, and if love could devise something new, we welcomed it. We entered on each joy the more eagerly for our previous inexperience, and were the less easily sated." I was familiar with the concepts of first base, second base, and beyond, but never had I realized there were stages of making love. I wondered if the scholarly background of Abelard and Heloise's physical grappling amplified its enjoyment. I was sure that it did: more educated minds must find more interesting ways for making love. After all, Abelard wrote about "something new." What *new* was there? More important, how could I find out about it?

In the thirteenth century, the French writer Jean de Meun included the story of Peter Abelard and Heloise in his best-selling poem *The Romance of the Rose*. De Meun used their letters (a translation of which he also published, separately) to illustrate that true love exists best outside of the shackles of marriage. De Meun applauded Heloise—"the intelligent and well-read young woman, who loved truly and was truly loved"—for her explicit rejection of marriage, quoting from one of her letters to Abelard, "If the Emperor of Rome, to whom all men should be subject, deigned to marry me and make me mistress of the world, I call God to witness that I would rather be called your whore than be crowned mistress."

Citing Heloise's repeated admonitions to Abelard that their scholarly studies as well as their sexual pleasures were best served by limiting the time they spent together—"their joys were more agreeable and their pleasures heightened when they saw one another more rarely"—de Meun concluded their sad tale with a flourish: "If Peter [Abelard] had believed her, he never would have married her." And so would have saved himself a lot of pain.

Since publication of *The Romance of the Rose*, the once-guarded letters of Abelard and Heloise have been shared and represented (and misrepresented) through poems, paintings, plays, books, movies, and even a musical. Abelard and Heloise have fan pages on Facebook with hundreds of followers, and dozens of YouTube videos have been dedicated to them.

It is the authenticity of expression—Heloise's lusty love!—that has drawn so many devoted followers to the couple. This authenticity was possible only because of the guarantee of privacy under which the letters were written.

The guarantee of privacy was particularly important for Heloise. Once she'd taken the vow of monastic life, she enjoyed a reputation for sanctity and goodness. She was viewed as a woman who had been corrupted by lust (and a man) but then reformed through faith. In the world in which Heloise functioned, playing the role of both dedicated abbess and spiritual leader, the truth about her sexual and religious feelings, if revealed, would have caused her to lose her place in that world. Heloise could have been stripped of her office, shorn of all powers, and tossed out on the street.

Heloise felt safe enough in the privacy granted by a letter to reveal to Abelard continuing love and desire, her aching nostalgia for past sexual pleasures, and her lack of religious conviction. Had she kept a journal, those same thoughts might have appeared in her daily writings. But what is written in diaries is not the same as what is written in letters. Letters are both private and shared at the same time, a hidden admission between the one who writes and the one who receives.

Certainly there are letters written quite deliberately to be shared, and correspondence specifically designed for a much larger audience—or, in the case of Peter Abelard, to a just slightly larger audience. After writing his letter of consolation to the depressed friend, he made sure that Heloise received a copy of it. Did he mean it as a sort of apology? Or as a warning that his rendition of their love story—and his alone—would be the accepted account of their doomed love affair?

Perhaps the letter of consolation was his way of writing their history *his* way, a form of wishful thinking that left Heloise far behind him. Or maybe Abelard was seeking to promote Heloise's reputation for sacrifice and piety, thereby protecting her. His letters could be seen as a medieval version of spin doctoring, done to further the cause of reputation preservation (both his and hers). But the power of the spin relied upon the veracity of the letter, and the veracity depended upon the cloak of privacy under which it was written.

Where does such a cloak of privacy, a guarantee of concealment, come from? We expect our letters to be kept private, we do what we can do to keep them private, and we have done so for millennia. The philosopher Cicero, living in Rome two thousand years ago, understood that there were two kinds of letters, personal and public, and that both served functions of communication: "I have one way of writing what I think will be read by those only to whom I address my letter, and another way of writing what I think will be read by many."

Cicero knew that certain measures had to be taken to ensure the privacy of those letters he deemed personal. He used only trusted messengers to send his private letters, and wrote the most secret parts of his missives himself, without using a scribe. And yet with friends, Cicero depended upon honor alone as the guarantee of privacy. When Mark Antony, in an effort to ridicule

Cicero, read one of Cicero's letters out loud and in public, Cicero took this as proof of Antony's venality and treachery.

Events proved Cicero right: within months, Antony's henchmen killed Cicero. Cicero's last words were, "There is nothing proper about what you are doing, soldier, but do try to kill me properly." Does treachery operate on a slippery slope? Will a man who exposes the contents of a private letter today engage in murder tomorrow? Perhaps not, but Cicero's story would argue that betrayal of privacy leads to even worse acts of treachery. Protect the sanctity of letters, and forestall far more heinous crimes from being committed.

In 1578, Sir Philip Sidney of Kent, a poet and soldier, became convinced that his father's private secretary was reading the letters he wrote to dear old dad. Infuriated, he sent a missive to the secretary warning him against such perfidy and offering this promise: "If ever I know you do so much as read any letter I write to my father, without his commandment or my consent, I will thrust my dagger into you."

While we may keep our daggers sheathed in the present day, the threat of punishment still serves to protect the sanctity of letters. Tampering with mail anywhere in the United States gets you years in prison and half a million dollars in fines; in some countries, including Mexico and Brazil, the privacy of correspondence is a constitutional right and its violation an infringement of civil rights.

Once they've arrived at their destination, letters are protected through measures as simple as hiding or destroying the missives (after they've been read, of course). Letters also can be legally stored away from prying eyes; Georgia O'Keeffe requested in her will that the love letters exchanged between her and Alfred Stieglitz remain off-limits for twenty years following her death, a common practice among the more famous letter writers.

The privacy of letters also can be secured through warnings, as in the words James Seligman's mother scribbled on certain envelopes. "Nobody to read this," she wrote across one such envelope, containing a letter James had written to her in August 1923, while vacationing in Deauville, France. Who exactly was she shooing away?

I have to admit those words enticed me to open the envelope with even greater urgency. What would Cicero have thought of me? But I reasoned that all interested parties had long passed on, and that my love for James would protect whatever I found inside. Indeed, what I found was a bit disappointing (fitting punishment for a reader of a letter marked "private"). The letter related some gossip about cousin Peggy Guggenheim, "chaperoning a weird-looking man who may or may not be the father of her child."

If James's mother didn't want anyone (including me, a person she never could have imagined) to read these letters, why didn't she just destroy them?

Perhaps that shared moment between herself and her son was worth preserving, to revisit when she felt James to be far away and out of touch. There are many examples of love letters, personal and revealing, that might have been better off destroyed, but who can bear to erase proof of love, when that might be the only talisman left to declare its existence?

Love letters are the ones we tend to protect most against inquisitive eyes. After all, what can be found in a love letter is often so revealing that widespread knowledge of the contents could prove embarrassing at best, and damning at worst (look to Heloise). In writing a love letter, we allow decorum to fall away: rules are bent, boundaries erased, lines bounded over with full expression of need, desire, and adulation. Only under a cloak of privacy can such letters be written—and saved.

I've saved the letters written by Jack to me in my green trunk. A favorite is one written early in the morning of the first day of the year 1993. Written on small square desk notes, page after page, he ended his letter with the words "You believe in hope, and you are the hope of this drunken fool, Happy New Year my darling."

We'd been married eight months and our first child was due eight months hence. Hope in a letter, and love that has lasted through three more kids, a few more drunken nights, and so many Happy New Years.

Preserver of the family love letters, I fervently hope that the love letters from my past have been burned by former boyfriends (and crushes). But if such letters do resurface somehow and somewhere, I can say those letters were written with honest intent and sincere love underscoring every word—and that I was utterly dependent upon the cloak of privacy I assumed in writing them.

Rebecca Primus and Addie Brown lived in Connecticut in the 1800s. Rebecca was from a prominent black family, well educated and firmly grounded, and she enjoyed a certain level of prestige and prosperity in her community. Addie was from a very different background, her family life unstable and her early education marginal. Born in New York City, she came to Hartford in the mid-1850s to work as a servant in a number of boardinghouses and private homes.

Addie may have lived with Rebecca's family when she first came to Hartford, as the Primus family was in the habit of welcoming newcomers to the city and helping them find employment. Hartford at the time did not have a large African-American community, but it was a very cohesive one. It was just as active socially and politically, through the Hartford Freedmen's Aid Society and the Prince Hall Masonic Lodge, as it was religiously, with large black congregations found at both the Congregationalist and Methodist churches.

Addie and Rebecca became close friends, enjoying each other's company. Addie was lively and sassy, quick to complain but just as quick to exclaim with joy over a new bit of gossip or notice of an upcoming get-together, while Rebecca was more reserved and steady, a source of inspiration to young Addie. When Rebecca went off to Maryland after the Civil War to work as a teacher for newly freed former slaves (and where she would build a school and meet her future husband), the women stayed close through letters.

While Rebecca's letters to Addie have never been found, Addie's letters were saved and are now preserved in the archives of the Connecticut Historical Society. I drove up to Hartford to read the letters on a cold winter's day, an hour-and-a-half drive from my home. I arrived just as the library of the Historical Society was opening up. I approached the library desk with quiet excitement, my hand clutching the request slip for the boxes of Primus family letters.

"You may sit here," the librarian told me, gesturing to a small desk equipped with a pad of paper and a pencil. "You must use our notepads and only pencils are allowed around the documents." I nodded my agreement.

Two cartons were brought out for me. Sitting down, I gently tugged loose the first of the manila folders. I opened the folder; a piece of pale yellow paper slid out onto the table. It was lined in blue and measured about eight by nine inches around. The script was so fine it seemed to be calligraphy to my modern eye. Each letter of each word was carefully shaped, slender and strong, forming paragraphs that flowed across the page, sinuous and appealing.

I held the paper lightly in my hand and read the words. Just a thin wisp of yellow, it carried all the cares of Addie Brown, written out for her beloved friend on a hot summer day. Brown had written from her boardinghouse in Waterbury, with Primus far away in Hartford. The distance between the two was causing pain to young Addie: "I really did not know what to make of your long silence. I came to the conclusion that you had forgotten me. I was more than pleased to receive your long looked for letter and at last it arrived . . . I love you." To see those words, shaped so long ago and yet still so fervent, was like holding something alive, breathing and warm, in my hands.

The strong friendship between Brown and Primus was well known among their friends and family. Addie was often treated like a member of the Primus family, invited to events and reunions of visiting relatives. But the private letters exchanged between the two reveal a physical and deeply erotic element to their relationship: "O my Dear friend how I did miss you last night I did not have any one to hug me and to kiss . . . no kisses is like yours." Addie recalls time spent with Rebecca, "breathing the same air with your arm gently drawn around me my head reclining on your noble breast in perfect confidence and love . . . what would I not give at this moment to be with or near you my soul longs for it."

Addie vows to improve herself to impress Rebecca. She reads more and becomes more religious as well: "Dear Rebecca I am now going to inform you of something that you long desire that is this I have found a Friend this is Jesus." And yet we hear little about the new friend in further letters, and much about social occasions ("merriment now to chase away the sadness"), along with the heavy burdens borne by a house servant and seamstress ("I feel realy low spirited I sew all the week"). And always, Addie writes of her longings for Rebecca: "Dear bosom . . . happy I was, last night I gave any thing if I could only have layed my poor aching head on your bosom."

As the months and years pass, Addie's letters show more punctuation and fewer mistakes in spelling, and her vocabulary, always strong, grows even more evocative in expressing her feelings for Rebecca. Her handwriting remains exquisite (except when she is very tired) and the fresh and lovely phrasing of love and devotion is as strong as ever: "Rebecca I want to tell you one thing that is this if I went without eating for two or three days and then a person was to bring me something to eat and a letter from you and they say that I was only to have one or the other I would take the letter that would be enough food for me."

On another day she writes, "Dearest friend and only Sister I will never doubt your love for me again you say you put my picture under your pillow I wish I had the pleasure of laying along side of you." And yet another: "I wish I could exchange pen and paper for a seat by your side and having a pleasant chat with thee. It will be many months before I will have that pleasure so I must resort to my pain."

As I read through the letters, a classic love story unfolded, with all its elements of pleasure, denial, fear, and joy. One letter that Addie sent had been folded over and over, as if Rebecca had kept it with her always, in her pocket. It is a short note and underneath her signature, Addie added a postscript: "Except [accept] a secret kiss I will imprint on here so look good you may perchance find it." I did not see the imprint of the secret kiss but I placed my finger there to sense its touch.

The love story ends tragically. Addie dies too young, at the age of twenty-eight. Rebecca scribbles across the envelope of her last letter: "Addie died at home, January 11, 1870." Rebecca would live on without Addie for another sixty-two years, more than twice Addie's entire lifetime. When Rebecca died, at age ninety-five, the one hundred and fifty letters she'd received from Addie were found among her family papers. For all those years, she had saved the letters of her friend and lover.

What love story will be revealed to generations hence, via the letters I have saved, the secret missives shared with my husband? I tend to write more poems than actual letters to my husband: "The house fell down / The kids ran away / The cat threw up / The creditors say 'pay' / The bank went bust / My sister's moving in / My knee is shot / And in my arm, they've put a pin / It's raining outside / There's ice on the vine / But all that doesn't matter / If you'll always be mine."

While on a business trip to London years ago, Jack wrote to me every day, sometimes only a line—"the geese ain't squawking yet" (reference to the poem by W. H. Auden about loving someone until "the seven stars go squawking / Like geese about the sky)"—but more often he wrote longer scrawlings of love and absence: "The last Valentine's Day of the Millennium—and we are an ocean apart. I would give anything to hold you now or to see the sweet smile that lights my heart."

Written in the privacy of his room at the Savoy Hotel, and in the privacy of his lightened heart. And shared with me.

4

Just for Me

Hundreds of books in a library
Thousands of freckles on a face
Millions of Memories going by right now
But no matter what,
There's only one unique mother for me.
> —*Card written to me*
> *from Peter, age eleven*

Gertrude Stein and Alice B. Toklas had been a happy couple for years, living together in Paris and holding lively salons at their apartment on the rue de Fleurus, when Samuel Steward popped into their lives. Stein was an established writer, and Steward was an aspiring one. He wrote a letter to Stein in 1932, setting in motion a decades-long correspondence. Before they ever met in person, Stein assured Steward, "When we do meet we meet but we do meet as we have met and it always has been and will be a pleasure." Letters had begun their friendship, and sealed it.

Sam Steward was originally from the Midwest. He was by all accounts a beautiful and slight young man, known both for his intelligence and his indefatigable curiosity. He was also purpose-driven and determined, traits most likely picked up from the three maiden aunts who raised him after his mother died. The aunts ran a boarding-house in the small town of Woodsfield, Ohio, where Steward grew up among boarders and spinsters. When it was time for Steward to go to college, two of his aunts up and moved to Columbus, setting up a boardinghouse close to the campus of Ohio State so that Steward could con-tinue on with his studies, even through the years of the Great Depression. Steward secured a PhD in English in 1934 and began his career teaching at a small school in West Virginia.

From an early age, Steward understood that his sexual preference for men was both a curse and a boon: a curse because of the stigma attached to homosexuality, and a boon because of the adventures and pleasures afforded him—and he was determined to find as many such adventures as he could. Steward was an open seeker of experience, as wild and varied as possible.

Always a record keeper, Steward kept journals and detailed notes of his many sexual escapades. In July 1926, just one day after turning seventeen, Steward sought out Rudolph Valentino at his hotel in Columbus, hoping for an autograph. Having given the autograph, the aging film star asked Steward what else he wanted. Steward responded,

"I'd like to have you." In the end, Steward took away not only the autograph of the film star but also a snippet of his pubic hair. Steward enshrined the hair in a kind of reliquary that he kept on his bedside table for the rest of his life. The reliquary is now held in a private collection in Rome. (I just cannot stop wondering: who would collect such a thing?)

But Gertrude and Alice knew nothing of the reliquary or of Steward's sexual escapades. In the elegant letters he wrote, he told them about his teaching and professed his admiration of Stein's writing. Praise is always a good way to greet an author, and Stein replied with enthusiasm to Steward's effusive notes. When he sent her a copy of his 1936 novel, *Angels on the Bough*, she offered him genuine praise back—"I like it I like it a lot, you have really created a piece of something"—and encouraged him to keep writing.

Angels on the Bough was considered racy at the time, telling the story of six bohemians from Ohio who struggle through the Depression exploring love, sex, and politics. The trustees of the State College of Washington, where Steward was teaching at the time, were scandalized by the plot and characters of the book, and Steward was fired. Stein responded to the news by urging Steward to write more and more—"go on and do another"—and extended a long-awaited invitation: "you are coming over are you not" (punctuation was eschewed by Stein). Indeed he was "coming over," he wrote back to her. In August 1937, Steward made his first trip to Europe.

Stein was not the only literary figure Steward had courted by correspondence, and he had more than a few invitations from writers to drop by during his grand tour of Europe. In fact, much of the activity in Steward's life, both as a sexual adventurer and as a writer, was prompted by the writing of letters. But it was the correspondence with Stein and Toklas that mattered the most, and he was eager to make his way to them (after stopovers in London and Paris, and dalliances sexual and otherwise, including a tryst with the decrepit Lord Alfred Douglas, ex-lover of Oscar Wilde).

Steward arrived in the small town of Culoz, close to the Swiss border in southern France, on a hot day in August. Gertrude Stein and Alice B. Toklas were at the station to greet him, Gertrude calling out, "Damnation! There he is, it's Sammy himself." With Stein and Steward in the front and Toklas in the back filing her nails, Stein drove to the somewhat sagging but still glorious country house that she and Toklas rented in the hills of Bilignin. The house was surrounded by vine-yards and orchards; Mont Blanc rose off in the distance. Steward easily settled into the routine at Bilignin: early walks with Stein, abundant meals prepared by Toklas, and field trips through the countryside. Stein and Toklas drove Steward all over their adopted valley, posing and making him pose for photos wherever they went. Back home from their adventures, Stein would set Steward to work in the garden or suggest another walk up into the vineyards.

Every evening before bed, Steward took copious notes of all that had happened during the day and took secret tipples from his hidden bottle of cognac. It is from those notes that Steward wrote his memoir, *Dear Sammy*. He included in the memoir an assortment of the letters that made up the years of their mutual correspondence.

A good friend sent me the book *Dear Sammy* a few years ago. What I found was a loving and unique relationship instigated, nourished, and exemplified by a voluminous correspondence. And even better, I discovered just how singular a letter can be. Each and every letter exchanged between Steward, Stein, and Toklas was so distinctly his or her own. I could tell which Stein had written, which were from Toklas, and which were from Steward.

Just days after he left them in the summer of 1937, Stein wrote to him, "We liked you before hand and we liked you a lot more after." From that letter on, Steward became "My Dear Sammy," a term of endearment and of loyalty; Steward returned both. Over the years that followed, hundreds of letters would pass back and forth among the three, a blitz of keen interest and blatant gossip and fervent shared affection.

Thanks to an introduction from Stein, Steward met Thornton Wilder in Zurich that first summer after leaving Bilignin. Wilder would become another lifelong correspondent with Steward, as well as an on-again, off-again lover. I've read many of the letters Steward and Wilder wrote back and forth to each other, but it is the letters exchanged among Stein and Toklas and Steward that I choose to reread, again and again. Why? Because the contrasts and confluences of those three different writers draw me into their circle of friendship. Reading their letters makes me an honorary member of their society of conversation, creation, and good times. As much as the letters drew the three together, they draw me to the three.

I imagine myself walking the hills behind the house at Bilignin, and working in the garden side by side with Alice B. I go to parties at the house of the writer Daniel-Rops and hang out with the surrealists Yves Tanguy and André Breton. Then I travel home to Connecticut and write letters back to France, thanking my hosts for the great times I had. And I know that those letters would be just as unique as the real ones shared by Steward, Toklas, and Stein.

Stein disdained all punctuation in her letters: "Everyone knows a question is a question so why use a question mark. And commas, they help you put on your coat and button your shoes for you and anyone can do that. But I believe in periods because after all you have to stop sometime." She was, however, lavish with love: "We love you a lot and you are a sweet Sammy." Steward tended to be cerebral in writing to the two women and clever, rendering lovely and often quite emotional descriptions: "The lake is only a hundred yards away . . . the other night at midnight I did walk down there, it was blowing and wild . . . You stand on an embankment overlooking darkness and see no line between sky and water but only a sullen void with whiteness fretting and circling at your feet, in a thin crisping edge of foam, and the winds are wild and roar in your ears, and at such moments you believe you can do anything in the world."

Toklas began many of her letters to Steward with an apology for not writing sooner: "It's a long too too long a time since you've heard from [me]"; and toward the end of her life, as she became more and more Catholic, she offered benedictions in her sign-off: "Bless you dear Sam—God and all the Saints." And like Steward, she also could write the most beautiful descriptions: "It rained the purest most direct from Heaven rain yesterday I've ever seen—with not as much as moving a leaf—each drop knowing its place went directly to it and all day they fell with precise regularity. It was English not French poetry."

The three correspondents wrote to each other in manner and form unlike how they wrote to others. Stein wrote often to composer Virgil Thomson, another gay and artistic man who visited the two women frequently. Stein even collaborated with him on putting some of her work to music. Yet, while her regard for him is clear, her letters to him are never effusive in love; they are contained (even slightly punctuated!) and gracious with sign-offs like "Best to you" and at most "Lots of love." And when Toklas eventually came around to liking Thomson (she had not liked him on first sight), she treated him kindly but not with the kind of mothering and worrying and loving that she expressed toward Steward.

The letters Stein and Toklas wrote to Thornton Wilder bore greater similarities to the ones they wrote to Steward, in terms of the loving and mothering tones. They also gave Wilder, like Steward, a diminutive name of affection— "Thornie," in Wilder's case. Nevertheless there are distinct differences in their letters to dear Thornie. The two women often wrote together to Thornie, whereas the letters Stein wrote to Steward were from her, and her alone. Likewise, Thornie usually wrote to the two women together, his two "Angels ever Bright and Fair," while Steward wrote individual notes to Stein and later to Toklas.

Steward was a dogged correspondent, resolved

to write what the recipient would want to read. To Stein and Toklas, he wrote of writing and reading, of love and anguish and resolution, and even failure. They were like adoring mothers, and he fed their adoration, while feeding upon their advice: "You are right, the question of being important inside oneself can either cause or cure a lot of trouble . . . I will be whole again and write and do the things I want." To others (men), he wrote of ardent physical love and desire, and quite often he wrote pornographic tomes of sexual wishes and remembrances (one correspondent insisted he sign his letters with a female name, to avoid any trouble).

A written letter is always a one-of-a-kind document, a moment in time caught on paper, thoughts recorded and sent on, a single message to a special recipient. Nonforwardable to any other person, addressed as it is to one person and one only, and fully traceable back to the writer, by virtue of the handwriting, the stories told, and the terms of endearment used.

Choice is part of the singularity of letters. Steward had a vast secret life made up of hundreds of sexual liaisons, as well as a whole side career (a successful one) of writing pornographic literature. He shared certain aspects of his life with his beloved ladies in France but hid others. A number of times Steward ended up in the hospital after searching out new sexual experiences; Steward did let the women know about his injuries, but he claimed they were due to auto accidents—and not the result of being beaten up while looking for sex in back alleys.

Steward turned thirty during his 1939 visit to Bilignin, and Stein celebrated by a poem to him: "All Little Sammy . . . On his birthday." Toklas had promised a chocolate torte in addition to the poem but the torte never materialized, there were visitors coming in from Chamonix, but no matter. The poem was what he wanted, and cherished, along with the friendship, and the shared experiences.

Steward had to cut short his visit to Bilignin that summer, as threats of war roared through Europe. He made it back to the United States on a last-minute berth on an ocean liner, writing to Stein from his bunk, "A whole oceanful of love to you and a hope that we can see each other next year when all is calm again."

The wartime letters between Stein and Toklas and Steward were often delayed and sometimes lost. And yet the trio kept writing. When Steward's brother-in-law was killed serving in the army in Germany, Stein sent a letter of condolence to Steward, in which she promised, "Sure some day you will come back, there are lots of new ones, but you will be a welcome old one, you bet."

Despite Stein's promise, Steward would never see her alive again. She died in 1946, one year after the war ended, after undergoing surgery for stomach cancer. Toklas sent the news to Steward by letter. Steward was devastated.

He immediately sent his condolences to Toklas. She responded equally quickly: "there came back to me the really good time you had given Gertrude . . . Gertrude was the happiest person that ever was but you found a way to give her a new pleasure—and so I will always love you." Three very different people, joined by their mutual affection. Now there were two, and the letters continued.

While Stein was alive, Toklas's letters to Steward had been businesslike, more concerned with setting up meetings and visits than with sharing confidences. But after Stein's death, Toklas began to write very long and personal letters to Steward, letters not only about her memories of Stein but also detailing the ways in which she hoped to keep Stein's legacy strong. She also wrote about her own growing ties to Catholicism and encouraged Steward to become more religious.

Steward responded to Toklas with his own long and personal missives, telling what he was reading about, thinking about, and writing about. When he thought such a promise would cheer the ailing Toklas, he feigned a new allegiance to the Catholic Church and indeed, Toklas wrote back, "What wonderful good news . . . You are my sweet Sam."

For fourteen years, Stein, Toklas, and Steward wrote back and forth to one another, and for another twenty years, Toklas and Steward exchanged letters. Steward visited the aging Toklas in Paris, most frequently at Christmastime. His last visit to her was in December 1966. Toklas died in March, just short of ninety years old, and was buried beside Stein at Père-Lachaise cemetery, in a corner due north and slightly east of the joined grave of Abelard and Heloise.

"Rose is a rose is a rose is a rose" is one of Gertrude Stein's most famous lines and appears throughout her works, both prose and poetry. She uses the phrase to convey the idea that a thing, whatever that thing is, represents both the reality of that thing and the emotions and history and repercussions that go along with it. Take Stein's phrase and apply it to letters themselves. A rose is just a rose (which is perfect enough), much as a letter is just a letter, perfect enough for me. But it is also so much more.

Held in Alaska every summer for years, the Midnight Sun Writers' Conference draws writers from all over to meet, talk, and cavort under the never-setting summer sun. As writer Bobbie Ann Mason described it, when she attended in the 1980s, "You have the feeling that you have all day to get something done and that the day will never end." When the annual conference wrapped up in 1979, the poets William Stafford and Marvin Bell made a commitment to each other.

Stafford was sixty-five years old the summer he attended the Midnight Sun Writers' Conference and Bell was thirty-five. Stafford was a pacifist—he had been a conscientious objector during World War II, when he was sent to spend his wartime service in the forests of Arkansas, California, and Illinois—and as he described himself, he was "quiet of the land," listening with all his senses to what nature had to tell him and finding inspiration in what he heard. Bell, who served in Vietnam in the sixties, was also against war (in the last ten years he has published a number of works protesting the war in Afghanistan and Iraq) and was, like Stafford, a poet deeply in tune with the physical world: "Ideas spring from the senses."

Stafford and Bell were determined to continue to share what had begun between them while hanging out under the midnight sun of Alaska: an ongoing dialogue about experience. They would continue that dialogue through letters. As Stafford explained, "The stray feelings and thoughts, the strange little bonuses when you push words toward each other, the easy to neglect but inwardly significant events of your life—keeping in touch is a way to welcome those happenings, to link and confirm them, there on the page, between friends."

The mode in which they decided to correspond was through poetry. In an exchange of poems, they would express their daily musings or doings or desires. And so for two years Bell and Stafford corresponded with poetry, forty-four poems in all. As Bell wrote in a book of the poems they later published, "Everything there is to say about poetry is contained in the word 'correspondence.'" And, he added, such a letter "brightens the mail."

How wonderful it must have been to find a poem in the mailbox. The length and rhythm of the poems varied, and sometimes weeks passed before an answering poem arrived. But each poem fed off the one before, creating both a conversation and a unique communication of ideas. Some poems were hopeful and bright, like this one by Bell entitled "Slow":

> I like runs that take a hill in one direction,
> pass a body of water,
> go down one street no one knows,
> and find a breeze . . .

While others were more somber and dark, like Bell's "Reflexes":

> Sometimes, you have to imagine the worst
> to prepare; the calm fire drill at school
> or the desperate decisions that come
> in the dark: which room, which child?

We fuzz it up with heroics, charades.
No one can picture the worst.

The poems exchanged between the two men did what letters do, re-create a moment or emotion in time, and share that moment with another. As Stafford wrote in one poem,

> . . . I pinch off a part of the story I know;
> toss it to you. And other parts to
> my mother, Belle, and my sister, Ruby.

Later, the poems would be shared with others, when the collection was published as *Segues, A Correspondence in Poetry*. But at the time of the writing, each and every poem-as-letter was created by one poet for just the other. In one of the poems sent by William Stafford to Marvin Bell, I find lines that offer the perfect encapsulation of letter-writing:

> For awhile, reading your lines, I ran
> on your trail so well I could never be lost.
> And sometimes when you turned I was
>   already
> there, your very best friend . . .

Edward Gorey is a cartoonist famous for his slightly creepy but thoroughly delightful cross-hatched drawings full of Edwardian atmosphere. He illustrated everything from TV opening titles (PBS's *Mystery!* series) to Dickens's *Bleak House* to T. S. Eliot's *Old Possum's Book of Practical Cats*, as well as writing and illustrating over one hundred of his own works. One of his drawings caught my eye last year as I flipped through a magazine and saw a reproduction of an envelope addressed to a location on Powder House Road Extension in Medford, Massachusetts. On the envelope was a drawing of a giant brown slug with many tentacles, peering curiously over an unwitting young woman dressed in a long, pink dress and carrying a parasol. The address on Powder House is inked in across the slug's spine.

Do slugs have spines? I wondered. And, *Where did this envelope come from? Are there more?*

A little research uncovered an amazing answer: yes, there were more, dozens of specially illustrated envelopes sent by Gorey to his friend Peter Neumeyer over a three-year span of time. The two men first met in the summer of 1968, when Neumeyer paid a visit to Gorey's Cape Cod home. Gorey had agreed to do the illustrations for Neumeyer's upcoming children's book titled *Donald and the . . .* , and their publisher had arranged for them to get to know each other during an afternoon sail.

But the outing on the water didn't prove to be an effective icebreaker, with both men remaining quiet and reserved. When the boat finally circled back to the dock, Neumeyer leapt nimbly, and with some relief, to shore. Gorey, however, slipped as he came out of the boat, losing his footing. As he headed into the bay, Neumeyer leapt to his rescue, saving Gorey from a fall off the pier but dislocating the illustrator's shoulder.

The ensuing wait in the emergency room at Hyannis Hospital thawed the mood between the two men. Stuck there for hours, they began to talk, not only about their upcoming collaboration but also about life. Gorey followed up the meeting with a letter, sent in a specially decorated envelope, and over the next few years, dozens more such jazzy envelopes made their way to Powder House Road.

Some of the envelopes are simply sweet, like the one with a blue lizard waving a yellow flag proclaiming Neuemeyer's name and address or the one of a white bat floating over a gray-colored envelope, holding in his little paws more banners, again proclaiming Neumeyer's address. There are also more elaborate envelopes: in one, a little yellow hamster has turned the crank on an old-fashioned record player, releasing in a puff of yellow smoke the words "MR PETER NEUMEYER 12, POWDER HOUSE ROAD EXT., MEDFORD, MASS. 02155." Another envelope shows the same old-fashioned phonograph floating on a sea of brown and purple waves, below a yellow sky. A tiny sea creature clings to the edge of the phonograph while from the speaker floats a red cloud containing Neumeyer's address, written (as always) in the unique Gorey gothic lettering.

My favorite envelopes feature a naked and chubby little baby. On the first envelope, the poor lavender-tinted boy is being dragged up to the sky by a Satan-tailed blue and red flying lizard; Gorey explains in tiny letters underneath, "Yet another infant carried off—how sad . . . in process of turning it blue with cold." Neumeyer wrote back about his wife's consternation over the tragic story and Gorey responded with an envelope showing the baby, now plump and healthy (but still slightly purple) and with magnificent wings protruding from his back, flying joyfully through the sky while pulling the bedraggled dragon by the tail.

Imagine the joy of sticking a hand in a rusty old mailbox in Medford, Massachusetts, and pulling out a multicolored fantasy created by Edward Gorey! Not all letters can be so fabulous, but most are written for one, and meant for one.

J. D. Salinger wooed eighteen-year-old Joyce Maynard through letters, sending his first note to her after reading her article "An Eighteen-Year-Old Looks Back on Life" in the *New York Times Magazine* in April 1972. Thrilled to receive mail from *the* J. D. Salinger, author of *The Catcher in the Rye*, Maynard wrote back to him. A correspondence between the Yale freshman and the fifty-three-year-old writer began.

Salinger's letters were alternately sweet and charming, offering compliments about her writing, her "gift." But Salinger also warned Maynard against fame, advising her not to fall prey to the promoters and feet-kissers that would be swarming around her in the publicity fallout from her article. In reading his letters, Maynard felt that Salinger was offering personal and focused counsel. Always having felt herself to be an outsider, a New Hampshire hick out of sync with the urbane sophisticates of Yale, Maynard was convinced that only Salinger, a Jewish kid from a Yankee town, really understood her. He accepted her outsider status, even complimented her for her otherness, and he was there for her just as she was. Bulimic and bewildered, beleaguered by agents and editors, Maynard turned more and more to the ambit of safety and intimacy Salinger created in his letters.

Within five months of Salinger's first letter, Maynard dropped out of Yale and moved up to Vermont to live with him. But her shared life with Salinger was not as sweet in person as it had been in letters. She was cold and hungry much of the time (Salinger followed a weird diet anchored by frozen peas and lamb patties), and their sex life was difficult (intercourse was too painful for Maynard to withstand). Maynard felt lonely and cut off from the world, and Salinger seemed increasingly irritated with her, becoming both criticizing and distant.

Maynard struggled to figure out how to get their relationship to work, still certain that Salinger was her soul mate. But during a late-winter trip to Florida in 1973, Salinger ended things between them. While they were lying out on the sands of Daytona Beach, Salinger instructed Maynard to pack up her things, first from the hotel room and then from the house in Vermont: "Don't forget to turn the heat down and lock the door after you, once you leave the house," he added. Eleven months after Maynard had received her first letter from Salinger, their relationship was over.

More than twenty years later, in the late 1990s, Maynard found out that she was not the only young woman whom Salinger had wooed through letters. In her 1998 memoir, *At Home in the World*, Maynard goes through the list of other women Salinger courted in correspondence: one woman had written to Salinger from England and the relationship had gone far enough for Salinger to fly over and meet her. A college girl from California wrote to Salinger and he wrote back, prompting another plane trip, this time from California to Vermont.

Salinger also began a secret affair in the 1980s with the actress Elaine Joyce by writing her a letter. Joyce wrote back to Salinger, a correspondence ensued, and within months they were spending time together, keeping their relationship hidden for years. Their liaison ended only when Salinger took up with a young woman named Colleen.

It was that relationship with Colleen—another one fomented through letters—that would hit Maynard the hardest. Maynard believes that Colleen and Salinger met on a bus in the late 1970s, exchanged addresses, and began writing back and forth to each other. According to Maynard, even as Colleen married and became mother to her husband's son, the correspondence with Salinger continued.

The husband didn't mind the letters, he explained to Maynard when she tracked him down in the 1990s. Maynard writes in her memoir that when Colleen left her husband, suddenly and without explanation, he made no connection to Salinger. But Maynard suspected Salinger had played a role. When the ex-husband mentioned that all he knew about Colleen was that she was living in Vermont, Maynard became certain.

She traveled to Vermont and found Colleen living with Salinger. Salinger and Colleen had married but Maynard didn't see a husband and wife: she saw a woman courted to Salinger's side through letters, just as Maynard had been. Maynard thought she had been one of a kind, but she was wrong.

The promise offered by letters of love is

profound. And its betrayal can be shattering. For Maynard, the betrayal personified in Salinger's letters to other women was devastating but it had one positive outcome: it finally freed her of her enthrallment.

The letters of Gary and Lisa Morris offer the counterbalance to the depressing story of Salinger and Maynard's epistle-sparked (and doomed) love. Gary and Lisa have been writing letters to each other every day for over twenty years. Every single day. By February 2011, the couple estimated they had written over eight thousand letters back and forth. What do they write about, given that they live together? They write about the big stuff: their feelings, money, God, what's on their "bucket list." Lisa explains the letter writing succinctly: "The whole purpose of the love letters is that it's a gift of love." An onliest gift, each letter, and one of a kind.

The writers Blanche Howard and Carol Shields corresponded for about thirty years. Their letters document not only their extraordinary friendship—supportive and loving and enduring—but also their successes and failures in writing. Shields won the Pulitzer Prize for *The Stone Diaries* in 1995—"New York was smashing, like the Academy Awards only high seriousness instead of glitter and glitz"—while a few other prizes eluded her, and Howard had success with her novels and plays, but frustration as well—

"My biggest worry is that when they find out how old I am, publishers might back off."

The women wrote to each other about the pressures and sorrows of family life; impending old age ("Another good thing about getting older. I've given up all pretense of being a well-rounded person"); and always, always the latest books they were reading: "am reading Angela's Ashes—half way through, but to my surprise not as entranced as the rest of the world seems to be."

Shields and Howard did not share every little tidbit of life with each other, nor were even the most momentous of occasions necessarily committed to paper. It would be months before Shields wrote to Howard about the breast cancer that would lead to her death; Howard revealed only slivers of the hardships she had coping with a husband suffering from Parkinson's disease. But the parts of their lives that Shields and Howard did share with each other were those parts especially chosen, one for the other, and very specially communicated. By letter.

Peter is no longer physically present in my daily life—absent from the morning rush, and our family dinner, and the late-night conversations putting off the end of the day and bedtime. But I still need to share my days with Peter, and I want to get back parts of his. Not the full story of his college life, but the part that he describes just for me. That his letter will be just part of the story is no condemnation of the medium. How Peter shapes and pares an event, creating it for specific consumption by a specific recipient (me!), demonstrates the unique vitality of letters. Singular in writing, and in receiving.

5

Proof Positive

Documents create a paper reality we call proof.

—*Mason Cooley*

When the baby of Charles Lindbergh and Anne Morrow Lindbergh was kidnapped on the night of March 1, 1932, a ransom note was left behind in the child's bedroom. Written in broken English and marked with a strange symbol of perforated red and blue circles, the note advised the Lindberghs to start collecting cash while promising that the child was in "gut care."

Eleven more ransom notes would follow, the final one leading Lindbergh to a cemetery in the Bronx, late on an April evening. Lindbergh walked along the gravestones, looking for the rendezvous spot, darkness deepening around him. Just when he was about to give up, a man emerged from the shadows. The man reached for Lindbergh's box of ransom money, fifty thousand dollars in marked treasury bills, and handed Lindbergh a piece of paper in exchange. Written on the paper were instructions for finding the child. Baby Lindbergh was being held on a boat named *Nelly*, lying at anchor off the coast of Martha's Vineyard.

The *Nelly* boat was never found, despite repeated searches along the Cape Cod island. Lindbergh himself took to the skies, flying in low loops over the coastal towns in an effort to find the boat and the baby.

On May 12, the baby's body was discovered just four miles from the Lindberghs' New Jersey home. Local and federal investigators redoubled their efforts to find the kidnappers. The written ransom notes were the place to start. FBI analysts and renowned handwriting experts examined the first note and the eleven that had followed. They all agreed that the same person had written all the notes, and that the writer was of German nationality but had lived in America for some time.

It was not until 1934 that the investigation into the kidnapping and murder of the Lindbergh baby finally had a breakthrough, when marked ransom bills were used to buy gas at an Upper East Side gas station. Bruno Hauptmann, a German man who had lived in the United States for over ten years, was tracked down through the gas purchase and arrested. He was found with ransom money in his wallet, and a search of his home uncovered even more.

At Hauptmann's trial for kidnapping and murder, handwriting experts testified for the prosecution. In dissecting the ransom notes and comparing them to samples of Hauptmann's writing, they looked not only to similarities in style but also at misspellings and punctuation peculiarities that appeared again and again in Hauptmann's writings and in the ransom notes. During his examination on the stand, Hauptmann could not explain away the similarities and how he even misspelled "signature" in the same way it had been misspelled in one letter sent to the Lindbergh home.

Hauptmann was found guilty in February 1935 and put to death on April 3, 1936. He protested his innocence until the end. His wife, Anna Hauptmann, would continue the fight to prove his innocence until her death at the age of ninety-five, in 1994.

Alternative theories of the kidnapping and murder abounded throughout the years of the investigation, trial, and execution of Hauptmann, and persist to this day. The evidence of the hand-writing, however, remains an obstacle to the alternative theories: eight different handwriting experts testified that the notes were written by Hauptmann, and subsequent experts, as recently as 2005, also found "overwhelming evidence" that all the notes were written by one person and that the one person was Bruno Hauptmann.

· · ·

Jack the Ripper killed five prosti-tutes over a period of three months in 1888 in Whitechapel, an impoverished neighborhood of London. Each murder entailed a more bloody and thorough disembowelment of the victim than the one before.

Hundreds of letters were sent to the police during the periods of panic that followed each gruesome murder, but most were deemed hoaxes and only a handful are believed today to be authentic; that is, sent by the Ripper himself. The genuine Ripper letters brag about the murders committed and threaten of grisly deaths still to come.

A slice of human kidney accompanied one of the authenticated Ripper letters. The testing that could be done in late-eighteenth-century London revealed that the person from whom the kidney slice was taken had suffered from Bright's disease. Kate Eddowes, a Ripper victim whose kidney was removed during the murderous rampage that killed her, was known to have suffered from Bright's disease.

Perhaps inspired by that kidney, Patricia Cornwell, the bestselling mystery writer, hired forensic experts to go through all the letters of Jack the Ripper, asking that they analyze the fragments of DNA that could be lifted from the papers, as well as the kinds of words and type of paper utilized by the person writing out the awful notes.

Cornwell had become convinced that Walter Sickert, a highly regarded artist of the late 1800s (the Royal Academy in London hosted a show of his works in 1992), was Jack the Ripper. Sickert painted a number of works displaying the underworld of music halls and prostitutes, and Cornwell found many of the images in Sickert's paintings to be eerily reminiscent of photos she had seen of the Ripper crime scenes. She obtained Sickert letters at auction and added them to the Ripper letters she wanted her forensic team to analyze.

What Cornwell's team found in its examination of the letters was that a watermark on one of the Ripper's letters (the mark of its manufacturer) was the same as that found on writing paper used by Sickert. In addition, the language used by the Ripper bears similarities to phrases used by Sickert in his correspondence. The name "Nemo," which the Ripper used repeatedly in his letters, was one of the stage names Sickert used during his acting days. The Ripper's letters also exhibit a number of doodles that were similar to doodles made by Sickert.

The DNA that Cornwell's investigators pulled off the letters matched the general pool of Sickert's DNA, but because Sickert was cremated, no exact match of his DNA can be made. By far, the more convincing evidence found by Cornwell is the writing similarities and comparable doodles in the letters of Sickert and of the Ripper. But although I love Cornwell's many mysteries, I feel this is one crime she has not solved to satisfaction. The letters of the Ripper may prove he was a monster—but *which* monster is a question that may never be answered.

In April 1836, Helen Jewett, a prosti-tute living in a luxurious Manhattan brothel, was killed by a hatchet blow to the head. Her bed, with her body in it, was then set on fire. In her room police found a chest filled with letters. The letters were mostly from clients, including one man who had asked that Jewett begin her servicing of him through correspondence, as he was too ill to travel to her room. Letters from another client, Richard Robinson, were also discovered.

Within days of the murder, Robinson, a young clerk working for a cloth dealer in lower Manhattan, was arrested at his boardinghouse. Witnesses had seen Robinson in Jewett's room on the evening of her death. In addition, an axe belonging to the shop where Robinson worked was found by a fence bordering the backyard of the brothel, and a cloak similar to the one Robinson had been seen wearing the evening of the murder was found on the ground nearby.

The murder of Helen Jewett became a press

phenomenon, boosting circulation for dozens of penny presses throughout New York City and also for the more established papers up and down the Eastern Seaboard. Differing versions of her past were offered up, stirring up the interest of all strata of society. Was she a poor victim, led down the path of indecency by bad luck and worse men? Or was she an evil temptress who got what she deserved?

The press, for the most part, portrayed Jewett as a beautiful young woman, known among friends and clients for her intellect, her sense of fashion, and for the letters she wrote and received. James Gordon Bennett, editor of the *New York Herald*, noted "last summer she was famous for parading Wall Street in an elegant green dress, and generally with a letter in her hand." A wildly popular print of her that began circulating after her death shows her heading off to the post office, a letter held in her dainty hand, ready to be posted.

Reporters tracked Jewett's origins to Maine, where she had been born to impoverished parents. After her parents died, she was taken in as a servant in the prestigious household of a judge. Numerous news stories reported that it was in the judge's household that she was either seduced or was the seducer in a sexual affair that would begin her spiral into prostitution. Whoever the man was, he eventually left her high and dry, and Jewett became damaged goods. To survive, she turned to selling her body, first in Boston and finally in New York City, where she cultivated high-paying clients and an elegant lifestyle.

Like Jewett, Richard Robinson was young and good-looking. The son of a prominent Connecticut family, he had been sent to New York City to learn a trade and mature into a man. He worked long hours as a clerk for the prosperous merchant Joseph Hoxie, lived in a boardinghouse not far from the store, and spent what little free time he had enjoying the entertainments of the flourishing city. It was at one of these entertainments, most likely an evening spent at a music hall, that Jewett and Robinson met, sometime in the summer of 1835.

From the moment he was arrested for the murder of Jewett, Robinson swore he was innocent. At first, public sentiment tended to favor him. After all, Robinson was a hardworking clerk and the son of a good Yankee family, whereas the witnesses against him were all people associated with the brothel and therefore deemed dissolute and unreliable.

Yet the character of Helen Jewett enthralled and eventually charmed the public. Newspapers poured out more and more detailed (and not necessarily accurate) accounts of Jewett's hard past, her recent state of elegance, and her potential for goodness. The details of her room were well publicized: amazed hordes read about her collection of books and fine writing paper, and the portrait of Lord Byron she had hung proudly on the wall. Jewett's feminine looks were touted as beyond compare, with reports in the press about her fine face and very dainty hands and feet.

Certainly there were those who claimed Jewett to have been coarse and vulgar, but the majority of the press, both in words and in drawings, showed her to be almost goddesslike. The editor of the *New York Herald* described her body in death as "polished as the pure Parian marble. The perfect figure—the exquisite limbs—the fine face—the full arms—the beautiful bust—all—all surpassing in every aspect the Venus of the Medicis." (All this despite the fact that the editor's only glance at her took place after she'd been set on fire and then autopsied, with her torso sliced open.)

From the start of their relationship, the sexual liaison between Robinson and Jewett took on the tones of a romantic courtship, albeit one bought and paid for. The letters Robinson and Jewett shared in the early days were full of love and longing and desire: "Here I sit . . . fresh from heavenly dreams of you. Nell, how pleasant it is to dream, be where you will and as hungry as you will, how supremely happy one is in a little world of our own creation." And Jewett wrote back, "Do you feel today as if you had been floored last night, or not; for my part, I feel literally used up, and mean to enjoy to its fullest extent, a state of single blessedness."

But not all was sunshine and joy. As the months passed, the couple began to fight with each other, both in person and in letters, and Robinson in particular seemed to commit acts for which he later begged Jewett's forgiveness: "No one can love you more than I do, dear Nelly; yet how strange, whenever I meet you I cannot treat you even with respect. You must think it very strange that I profess to love you so much and yet always treat you so harshly. Yet I have told you over and over again, that loving you as I do and not being able to see you, it makes me most crazy, and I have no control over my feelings, but Nelly you must forgive me."

Jewett would often antagonize Robinson but then follow up with her submissive appeals: "Dearest, you know I can forgive you anything . . . I am ill, I mean sick, sick at heart, and you do not know how unhappy I shall be until I see you."

At the time of Robinson's trial for murder, tightly presided over by Judge Ogden Edwards, little attention was paid to the correspondence found in Jewett's room. Judge Edwards did not allow the jury to see Robinson's letters demonstrating his desire to sever all ties with Jewett, and those warning her not to "betray" him. They were not allowed to see Jewett's replies, with her veiled threats as to the damage she could do: "Slight me no more. Trample on me no further. Even the worm will turn under the heel. You have known how I have loved, do not, oh do not provoke the experiment of seeing how I can hate."

Nor was Robinson's final letter to Jewett, written just a few weeks before her death, given to the jury to read. It is a chilling one: "I have read your note with pain, I ought to say displeasure; nay, anger. Women are never so foolish as when they threaten. You are never so foolish as when you threaten me. Keep quiet until I come on Saturday night, and then we shall see if we cannot be better friends hereafter."

My first thought in reading the letters between Robinson and Jewett was that Robinson, once he decided to be done with Jewett, was seeking to hide the fact they had ever been together. In November 1835, Robinson wrote to Jewett asking for all his correspondence to be returned, along with a miniature of himself he had given her, advising Jewett that "for the present, we must be as strangers" and "it is best for us to dissolve all connection."

But then I saw another reason for Robinson wanting the letters back. The letters the couple had exchanged were not only proof of his past adoration of Jewett and of their physical relationship, but also of his repeated bouts of obsessive anger. Robinson was seeking to destroy potential evidence before undertaking the planned deed of murder.

The only letter that Judge Edwards allowed the

jury to see was the one in which Robinson asked for the return of his writings and miniature. But he then summarily dismissed the letter as unimportant, stating that it had been written months before the crime and therefore was irrelevant. The judge reasoned to the jury that Robinson had no need to exert violence to secure what he wanted from Jewett. Jewett loved Robinson, according to Judge Edwards, and would have been happy to return whatever he asked of her, miniature and letters included.

But why did Judge Edwards refuse to allow the jury to see the letter written by Jewett in December 1835? In that letter she wrote, "You [must] never again pain me for asking again for your miniature, for heaven only can be my witness what pleasurable feelings it excites, while gazing upon it and recurring to the kind and generous manner with which you gave it to me." Jewett wasn't going to return the miniature or anything else to Robinson, not then, not ever. Anything he wanted he would have to take by force.

At the trial, a young woman who worked as a servant in Jewett's brothel testified that the miniature had been in Jewett's room the day before she was murdered, and a constable testified to finding the same miniature in Robinson's room two days later. Yet Judge Edwards advised the jury to disregard the servant's testimony and indeed any of the evidence offered by anyone affiliated with the brothel, as "not being entitled to credit unless their testimony is corroborated by others, drawn from better sources."

Judge Edwards then led the jury to his own conclusions that the cloak and the axe found close to the scene of the murder could both be explained away as having been left at another time or by another person. He instructed the jury that they could only convict Robinson if they felt it was beyond reasonable doubt that he had committed the crime; if any doubt persisted, the jury must acquit and "not immolate an innocent victim." In less than fifteen minutes, the jury returned to the courtroom and acquitted Robinson of the charge of murder.

Why did Judge Edwards work so hard to ensure an acquittal of Robinson? Perhaps because at the time of the trial, Judge Edwards's brother was governor of Connecticut and friends with Robinson's father. Edwards himself was acquainted with men engaging in licentious behavior; his father had been the model for a novel about a philandering scoundrel, and one of his favorite cousins, Aaron Burr, was famous for his romantic intrigues.

But no matter how Judge Edwards instructed his jury, in the court of public opinion Richard Robinson was condemned. By the end of the well-publicized trial, and in the following years as the letters between the two lovers became public, people on the street believed Robinson to be guilty of the murder of Helen Jewett. He was given the nickname "the Great Unhung" by a journalist for having escaped the punishment of hanging, and the nickname stuck. The letters between Helen Jewett and Richard Robinson may not have convicted Robinson in a court of law, but on the streets of New York City, he was viewed as the guy who got away with murder.

Fortunately, circumstances do not call for most letters of love to be used—or denied—in a court of law. Instead, we harbor our love letters while love flourishes, and destroy them when love leaves. A few letters may make it into divorce courts or criminal courts—as poor Oscar Wilde found out, when his love letters to Lord Alfred Douglas were used to put him behind bars for sodomy for two years—but most love letters are either treasured or burned, depending on how things work out. I've made a few piles of ashes myself over the years.

Today the only love letters I hold on to are from my husband—"You're the best one-legged friend a guy could ever have" (after my first knee operation)—and the letters of love I receive from my children. My youngest, Martin, often leaves me notes, scattering them throughout the house where I might find them during the day while he is at school, or leaving them on a chair beside his bed for me to find in the evening when he is asleep and I come in to check on him.

During our renovation of the town house on West Seventy-Eighth Street, my kids stuck their feet into the wet cement outside the basement door. The footprints, forever set in concrete, are proof that we'd been there, part of the history of that great old house. We had to leave the town house and our footprints behind, but the letters I carry with me, wherever I go. James's letters, and my children's letters. Proof of connection, mutual love, and shared lives.

A few years ago, I watched in shock as new friends gleefully toilet-papered the bushes in front of my house. It was just days before Halloween and Bev Stanley and her three daughters, all recent arrivals from England, had misunderstood an American Halloween tradition.

"What the hell are you doing?" I asked Bev, coming out of my front door onto the lawn.

"I am 'booing' you," she proudly proclaimed. Then she handed over a bag full of candy. "And here are your treats." Another American tradition misunderstood, but this one I could deal with.

It was not until we spent our first Boxing Day with the Stanleys that I understood what a push and pull immigration had been for Bev and her husband, Charles, coming from their old world in England into this new one, in southeastern

Connecticut. Not only did they have to catch on to local traditions and customs (we do not toilet-paper the houses of family friends), but they also had to hold on tight to old traditions, based on family practices going back through generations.

We were at their house on the day after Christmas, a day when traditionally the English handed out boxed gifts to their servants. We had dispensed with the gifts (none of us had servants) and brought instead bottles and bottles of wine, platters of food, and, as instructed, a family skit to be performed for all the other guests. After we finished off the big meal of turkey, potatoes, salads, cheeses, nuts, puddings, cakes, and cookies, it was time for the show. We performed our skits, a mishmash of rowdy dance routines and scenes from Dickens's *A Christmas Carol*. A cross-dressing Dad singing Cher tunes topped it all off. Now we were ready for the next event.

"Time to play Cocky Olly," Charles announced. The adults exchanged glances and raised eye-brows. Sounded a bit cheeky to us.

"No, no," Charles scolded, clearly disgusted by our filthy and somewhat inebriated minds.

"This is a game that has been played in my family for generations, and always during the holidays. My father grew up playing this game. He played in a house with twenty or so bedrooms, oodles of closets, and acres of hanging curtains"— the importance of these features was soon to be revealed—"but our present house will certainly do."

We all nodded, still oblivious as to what lay in store. Up came our eyebrows again as Charles reached behind a chair and pulled out a long iron fire poker, which he proceeded to brandish like a mad pirate. Or a mad Englishman.

"You all go hide and I must find you, one by one. When I find you, I will call out *'Cocky Olly'* and then your name, and you will be officially caught. When I have caught everyone, game over."

"What is that poker for?" one wide-eyed little boy asked.

"No idea, really," Charles admitted. "But my father always used a sword when he chased us around. The sword came from his uncle, from his time spent in India, and my father would stomp around the house, waving it over his head while chasing after us. I will do the same. Only with my poker." He whirled it over his head again.

The game began and complete hilarity ensued, with people of all ages hiding in all sorts of places, and yet still getting picked off one by one by the fearsome Charles. We poor player folk had the upper hand, nevertheless, because the rules of the game (yes, there are rules, rudimentary but absolute) provided that those players not yet captured could sneak down to the kitchen holding pen and rescue all those who had been caught.

Once rescued, we were free to hide again in laundry hampers, bathtubs, and clothes cupboards. The game finally ended when Charles dropped his poker on the floor and sank exhausted onto a couch.

We've gone back to the Stanleys year after year for Boxing Day. And every year we play Cocky Olly. One year I hid under a duvet and fell asleep, and was roused by Charles roaring in my ear that I had been caught (a bit too much eggnog on both sides). Then there was the year when my son George hid so well during Cocky Olly that nobody could find him at all, and he became frightened that he'd turned invisible. We tried to assure him it was just great hiding on his part. He wasn't convinced until we took him to a mirror to see the plain evidence.

As a boy, Charles's father had played the game every Christmas at Longleat, the huge family estate built in the sixteenth century and home to his uncle, the Marquess of Bath. In those days, the family's hunting dogs were put to use in ferreting out hidden children. Years later, Charles played the game during holidays, hiding out in the nooks and crannies of the old rectory farm where he grew up.

Whether Cocky Olly is played in a twentieth-century suburban colonial of less than epic proportions or in a sixteenth-century manor or in a farmhouse with hidden corners, the game is proof for Charles that he has a history. He was not just dropped down into America without a past or a family or a story (or two). He may be on his own in America, along with wife and kids, but all of them are buoyed by the family history that rests over in England.

Knowing of my obsession with letters, a few years ago Charles gave me two books. The first contains all the letters that the prime minister of England H. H. Asquith wrote to Venetia Stanley, Charles's great-aunt, in the early years of the twentieth century. Written over a period of three years, Asquith wrote over 560 letters to Venetia. In those letters, he shared details from all aspects of his life, political, social, and amorous.

And Lord Asquith was very amorous, expressing with great ardor, over and over again, his love for Venetia: "My love for you has grown day by day & month by month & (now) year by year; till it absorbs and inspires all my life. I could not if I would, and I would not if I could, arrest its flow, or limit its extent, or lower by a single degree its intensity . . . It has rescued me (little as anyone but you knows it) from sterility, impotence, despair. It enables me in the daily stress of almost intolerable burdens & anxieties to see visions and dream dreams."

As impressive as the collection of Asquith-Stanley letters is, it is the letters contained in the volume titled *The Stanleys of Alderley* that truly delight me. Edited by the novelist Nancy Mitford and published in 1939, the collection contains letters exchanged between Maria Josepha Lady Stanley and her daughter-in-law Henrietta Maria Lady Stanley from 1851 to 1865. But other Stanley family members pop up as well, putting in their own two cents in the form of letters. Henrietta's husband, Edward Lord Stanley, wrote to his wife because he was often away, spending most of his time off in London at the House of Lords or gallivanting around Scotland for two months every summer with friends (Lady Stanley was not invited). Letters from Edward and Henrietta's children, including Blanche, Johnny, and Lyulph, are also in the book.

As I read through the letters of the Stanleys of Alderley, it became clear to me that the matters of most vital importance to the family were the marrying off of daughters and the managing of sons. The first girl to be married was Blanche, the oldest daughter. A likely candidate for dear Blanche was David, the young Earl of Airlie. However, certain rumors of the earl's gambling habit worried grandmama Maria Josepha, while mother Henrietta fretted about his deafness: "I wish he were not so deaf, he only hears half one says," she wrote in a letter to her husband.

Nevertheless, the courting between Blanche and Airlie continued and, as Lady Stanley wrote to Edward, Airlie seemed very smitten with his

Blanche: "He never leaves her side for a moment, & she seems very well pleased, & they are now, between 12 & 1, sitting on the lawn with a book each, but I can see by the reflection in the window that he is not reading."

Reading the letter, I pictured the scene as described by Henrietta, recalling details from the Merchant Ivory movie *A Room with a View* to fill in the gaps. In the movie Cecil Vyse, played by Daniel Day Lewis, tries to woo Lucy Honeychurch, played by Helena Bonham Carter (whose great-grandfather happens to be the Asquith who wrote love letters to Venetia Stanley). Cecil comes to visit Lucy at home, and they sit together outside, lounging on a sloping green lawn. Cecil stares nervously at Lucy, shy and stammering, while Lucy looks bored. We in the audience know she is still mulling over the passionate embrace she received from George Emerson in a barley field outside of Florence.

"Blanche gets impatient & the more she is so the brusquer is her manner so that really I don't wonder a poor man cannot begin with sentiment," Lady Stanley wrote. "She rather talks to him as if he was to be civilized, she keeps giving him little passages to read."

So did Blanche Stanley have her own George Emerson off in the wings? Or was she putting off Airlie as a romantic tactic?

But unlike Cecil Vyse with Lucy, Airlie was

ultimately successful in his wooing of Blanche. Everyone was happy (and relieved) when the deal was finally done, and Airlie's promise that he would take Blanche to live in his castle in Scotland was the icing on the cake: "Blanche says it has always been her dream to be carried to a Castle . . . She is to have a Scotch terrier, a deer hound for the drawing room, a mastiff and retriever & I suppose everything else she fancies. They have now gone into the wood to cut their names on trees."

Early in the marriage of Blanche and Airlie, Lady Stanley wrote to her husband, "Blanche got a book today, *Hints to Mothers*, and we found Airlie reading it, so much the better for his ignorance is surprising." All ignorance must have been overcome, because Blanche eventually had five children. She would become grandmother to Clementine, the future wife of Winston Churchill, and great-grandmother to the famous Mitford sisters, including Nancy, who edited the Stanleys' letters.

There were slight hiccups in the marriage between Blanche and David. In a letter that Lord Stanley wrote to his wife in 1865, he traces the bumps in the road to one causative factor: Airlie's midlife crisis. The trouble all begins when a certain woman with "a vile American twang," called "senora" by Lord Stanley, comes to stay: "Airlie is more demonstrative to her than I ever saw him."

Lord Stanley later writes: "Airlie is infatuated [with the señora] & Blanche begins not altogether to like it & I think she can be jealous." Then Lord Stanley explains, "In short he [Airlie] has reached the dangerous age of 40."

What a deliverance it is when Lord Stanley can finally report to his wife, "The Senora is clean gone, Airlie resorted to his usual state of acquiescence, & Blanche I think is relieved."

With Blanche taken care of, it was time to manage sons. First there was Henry, the oldest son of Henrietta and Edward. Bored with England and fed up with English ways, Henry left England as a young man to travel extensively through the East, where he converted to Islam (answering the question raised in one of his father's letters, "Henry says he is going to Constantinople—what does he want to do in Turkey?"), and later married a Spaniard (when his father died, Henry became the 3rd Lord Stanley of Alderley and the first Muslim member of the House of Lords). There was no managing Henry, and little mention of him in the letters.

Then there was Johnny, younger brother to Henry and a hellion in school. At one point he was threatened with expulsion from the exclusive and elite Harrow. Lady Stanley shrugged off the accusations against him, writing to her husband, "To be sure impertinence to tradespeople is a small matter for public school." But Lord Stanley took a sterner position: "I have paid the school accounts . . . The amount is large and the profit seems to have been small. If Johnny won't work he must be shut up in his room & deprived of his dog."

Henrietta continued to defend the boy to her husband: "He is only a naughty troublesome idle boy, bad enough without giving the child vices he is not capable of." Yes, he was only naughty, troublesome, idle, and incapable of any interesting vices—so what's the problem?

Johnny chose to jump ship from school (probably a good idea) and at age sixteen went off to fight in the Crimean War (not such a good idea). Joining up with the Grenadier Guards of the British Army, he longed to "kill a Russian," and his letters from the Crimea are a mix of wry recounting of what must have been horrific circumstances ("I saw Colonel Yea buried, the body smelt very bad, I dined with Hibbert after") and moments of somber reflection: "Poor Field had Asiatic cholera, there was no hope he was quite black. I enclose a bit of his hair I thought of his poor mother . . . Do you mind breaking it to her."

Poor Johnny himself became quite ill with dysentery. Being cared for by Florence Nightingale (described by Johnny in a letter home as "that little old maid") was not enough; he was sent back to England to recover and then took off again in

120

service of England, this time to India, with more fighting on his mind and more jokes in his letters (it was his sword that Charles's father used to play Cocky Olly).

The youngest son, Lyulph, also wrote frequently to his mother, though grudgingly: "I really do not know what I am to write to you—if you can start a topic which we can dilate upon together I shall be most happy to write long letters to you. We do not agree on politics or on any other question—I cannot write long letters about my stomach like Johnny & as my digestion is quite right I do not suppose it would interest you to be told so . . . in such a case one hails the appearance of the fourth page like the sight of a harbour."

My favorite letters from the Stanley collection are the ones written by the two women, grandmother Maria Josepha and her daughter-in-law Henrietta. The women are witty and informed and quite sly, sharing opinions not only about social issues—"We have been very busy with the poor people all very thankful"—but also about politics. After all, they knew many of the players personally, including the man they called "Dizzy" (Benjamin Disraeli, who would be prime minister of England from 1874 to 1880), as well as Lord Palmerston (twice prime minister in the 1850s and 1860s), and Lord Granville (secretary of state for foreign affairs throughout the late 1800s).

Just as comfortably as they talk politics, the two

gossip about baby names—"Alice wishes me to tell you they have settled to name the baby Alexander St. George & she is sure you will think the name ridiculous—so do I"—and discuss literature: "I quite agree with you about *The Woman in White*—far too exciting for me—it made my heart beat very much." I wanted to jump into the conversation at that point, arguing for my favorite novel by Wilkie Collins, *The Moonstone*, and begging their opinions. It was hard for me to realize, engrossed as I was, that these letters were written over one hundred years ago—and that I would not get a response from the lively women I came to know through their letters.

Much as my own friends do today, the Stanleys of Alderley talked about real estate deals ("They gave 7000 for it"); house renovations ("took up the floor and found 69 dead rats! Fancy the smell"); and the blight of new technology ("How much more comfortable it was, *last* war, when the events were more slowly communicated—the *Electric* telegraph is I think a great nuisance keeping one in a constant ferment of apprehension & doubt what to believe").

Sarcasm is well employed. In writing to her husband, Lady Stanley offers, "Madame Valeski sent me a message to the effect that you were well amused at the Black Mount . . . How kind the world is to me, for fear that I should be in ignorance." But sorrow as well took its place in the missives, especially when the prince consort, Queen Victoria's beloved Albert, died in 1861: "The great calamity which has befallen the whole nation, is such that one cannot foresee how it may, perhaps must, affect every individual in the British Dominions—whether the poor Queen preserves her life or her senses through such a grief . . . it is dreadful to think what she must suffer."

The male correspondents in the collection of letters do not condescend to their female partners (other than Lyulph's adolescent rant against his mother for requesting that he write to her). In fact, there is so much sharing of ideas and opinions that the letters read quite modern, and are most certainly never boring. Likely Mitford's editing helped keep the letters lively. She writes in the introduction that "Lady Stanley's letters from Italy are of a length and of a boredom with which it would be cruel to inflict the reader." Thank you, dear Nancy.

I think Charles shared his family letters with me because he knew I would understand the proof such letters provide. Proof of where Charles comes from, not in terms of bloodline but in terms of family, not only in the past but also in the present. Just as playing Cocky Olly every year at Christmas helps Charles to ground himself in this brave new world of suburban Connecticut, the letters bolster his stance. The letters tell Charles not only what his forebears were up to all those years ago but offer solid supposition as to how much they would support Charles's efforts today to make sense of his life, lived in that most unlikely of places, America.

The Stanley letters affirm for me the bounty of family, serving up both attestation to their own peculiar frailties and strengths, and proof of the universal and enduring habits of gossip and chitchat, of sharing secrets and stating opinions, and always, always waiting for the next letter: "Perhaps I shall get a letter from you soon—but fancy 10 days without hearing," writes Lady Stanley to her husband. "It is raining hard. I must write, do not be vexed with me but pray let me hear of you."

In 1994, Robert Liely was driving from Napa Valley to his home in southern California, hauling boxes filled with family photos, letters, and other papers. In the center of the state, one of the boxes tumbled off the truck. Liely and his wife stopped to gather up its contents, scattered all over the side of Highway 101. But a California highway patrolman stopped and told the couple they could not park in that spot and had to move on. The Lielys drove off.

A few months later, Erick Gordon, a teacher from New York City, was driving along the same highway with a friend when she shouted at him to stop. She had spotted a goat standing on top of a cow and wanted a closer look.

Gordon parked his truck and he and his friend ventured out to see the goat. It was indeed standing on top of the cow, readjusting its stance for balance whenever the cow moved for another piece of grass. But the goat on the cow was not the most amazing find of their stop. At their feet they saw a letter, old and brown. When they picked it up, they saw it was postmarked fifty years earlier. And then they noticed another letter, and another, and another. Hundreds of letters, scattered in a line along the side of the highway.

The two gathered up all that they could, finding letters postmarked from the late 1890s through the early 1950s. All of the letters, three hundred in all, were addressed to an Ella Chase. Gordon later discovered that many of the letters were written to Chase from men serving overseas during World War II, all different men with different last names but each one referring to Chase as "mom."

Gordon brought the letters back to New York, using them as teaching tools for his writing students. He had them write stories based on the letters, using their imagination to fill in what was left unsaid. For twelve years Gordon wondered who Ella Chase had been and how she had come to have such a positive impact on so many young men serving overseas. He was able to uncover only tidbits of information about her. She had lived in Lomita Park, California, and run for political office in the 1940s.

In 2006, through a connection made by one of his writing students, Gordon found a fellow Chase-sleuth in NPR reporter Laura Starecheski. The hunt was on. Bit by bit, news clipping by news clipping, and by going through obituaries, census records, and court files, the history of Ella Chase was uncovered.

Chase had been unhappily married in the 1930s and sought a divorce in 1938 from her husband. His defense to the divorce action was that they had never been married in the first place. The case created a press sensation, headlines proclaiming "I Was Never Married" and "Mrs. Chase Near Tears Flays Mate." No divorce was granted. Four years later, Bellman Chase, the alleged husband, died on Christmas Day in San Francisco, drunken and beaten.

Ella Chase never claimed the body, having started a new life on her own, one that included her wartime correspondence with lonely and scared servicemen abroad. She received in return letters thanking her for her kindnesses, her caring, and her help: "I am so very grateful . . . thank you for changing the way I think about my life" wrote the boys from overseas.

In 1954 Ella died, leaving a grandson, Robert

Liely. Forty years later, Liely had lost his grandmother's letters while driving down Highway 101. Erick Gordon found them a few months later. Twelve years after that, Gordon tracked down Liely and returned the letters to him. Liely was relieved to find that his grandmother's letters had survived; proof of her existence returned to him. All due to a goat standing on a cow.

My friend Viveca has a letter her grandmother wrote to Viveca's father when he was imprisoned in a German camp during World War II. The envelope is chilling, addressed as it is to "Stalag II B." But the letter is sweetly domestic and largely ignores the implication of "Stalag" (prison camp). Instead, mother Van Bladel expresses the hope that her son Jean has received a pullover that was sent, advising him to take good care of all his clothes and to wear the sweater against the cold.

His mother wrote, "Have patience, little love" (my translation of "petit chou," which literally means "little cabbage"); all that was possible was being done on behalf of the imprisoned soldiers and she was sure that soon her son would be home, returned to Belgium and to his family: "What joy it will be to have you home again!" In the meantime, she advises, "learn some German." She closes by sending him a million hugs and all her love.

Jean Van Bladel was imprisoned for four months

and sent to work on a farm in the far reaches of Pomerania, harvesting potatoes on the estate of a wealthy German nobleman, and later threshing wheat. But by Christmas, he was repatriated to occupied Belgium and he returned to his family in Antwerp. The promises of his mother were proved true: there was great joy upon his return home! Viveca holds on to the letter her grandmother wrote as proof of the enduring love of family, and a reminder of the power of mothers to bring hope to their children; she never knew her grandmother, but through this letter, she feels the acquaintance has been made, and feelings have been shared and understood.

When I read old letters, I find comfort in seeing how familiar is the friendship, the love, the sharing of dreams and frustrations and disappointments. I feel easier in my own skin, seeing how those who came before me also muddled through in a mix of good intentions and false steps, and then found their footing again, with the help of friends and family.

The philosopher Thomas Carlyle wrote to Lady Stanley in 1864 to offer congratulations on the upcoming wedding of her daughter Kate: "Surely that is a hopeful and fortunate-looking thing! Sorry only that the bright young creatures are all taking wing so rapidly . . . But truly the epochs do chase one another at a frightful rate."

Time passes, and ever more rapidly as I grow

older. But letters remain. Most of us won't make it into the history books, like Lord Asquith and his love Venetia Stanley. But we can leave a part of ourselves behind in the letters we write, as proof that we were here.

6

Fly on the Wall

You can be a rank insider as well as a rank outsider.

—*Robert Frost*

In 1921, the *Oakland Tribune* published a short bit on their Women's Page about women seeking husbands, the writer noting that "I'd like to be a fly on the wall when the Man comes along" that will sweep a woman off her feet. The unknowable might become known, implied the author, through an insider's view of the moment a woman falls in love. The phrase "fly on the wall" stuck, becoming a national catchphrase for what we all secretly (and not so secretly) desire: an insider's view of other people's private thoughts, activities, and desires.

I love reading the letters of famous writers. I am a fly on the wall as the writer falls in and out of love, discards old habits and tries new ones, makes and loses friends, and finds inspiration. How reassuring it is for me to learn that the writer Franz Kafka suffered from writer's block—I know because he complained about it in a letter written in the early 1920s—or that the writer Dorothy Parker suffered from what she called "incompetence . . . all I have is a pile of paper covered with wrong words."

Edith Wharton wrote to Henry James from France in 1915. World War I was raging as she traveled to a small village close to the German line: "Only last Friday a number of people were killed . . . Luckily today they didn't happen to be firing, so we got there." She writes to him about the damages of war she has witnessed and of passing by the German lines "in full view"; she writes of climbing to the top of a ruined castle, going through "wattled trenches" to arrive on the summit at an artillery observation post. What does it say about Edith Wharton that after hearing about a man who "spent three days in his cellar, with wife and other womenkind, their house blazing over their heads, & the Germans shooting and torturing people . . . ," she writes most rapturously of the "magnificent" view? "In clear weather Metz is clearly visible, about 18 miles off." Perhaps I should not have been surprised, as she began her letter to James by stating "I don't dare write you except when I'm scaling heights or exploring trenches." The writer known for her acerbic view of New York high society turned her acute eye and sharp pen to the panorama of a ravaged Europe. And I was there, thanks to the letters she wrote.

In 1940, Richard Wright published his novel *Native Son*. In the decade that followed, he exchanged a series of letters with Dorothy Canfield in which he sought to explain the impulse and realities behind his writing: "Few whites know or suspect the enormity, depth, and meaning of the Negro problem in America, and I am convinced that the solution of this problem— I feel that it will eventually be fully solved—is destined to alter our nation and its people not a little, but all to our good."

Ten years later, Wright explains in another letter his understanding of the dilemma plaguing America: "The American people . . . their history, the very conditions of their lives and their mass production have produced something that has impressed me enormously—a terrible need for social relations in which their sense of individuality and their need for common human association can be fulfilled." Written in 1953, these words provide insight into the America Wright knew and I still live in.

There are letters that give an inside view to sorrow, as when Mary Shelley writes about the drowning of her beloved husband, the poet Percy Bysshe Shelley, off the coast of Italy in 1822. Shelley was just twenty-nine years old and was sailing from Livorno north to Casa Magni, the seaside home he'd rented with his wife and young child, when his boat went down in choppy waters.

"All that might have been bright in my life is now despoiled," Mary Shelley wrote to a friend after the drowning, and then described the circumstances of her husband's death: "A Fishing boat saw them go down—It was about 4 in the afternoon—they saw the boy at mast head, when baffling winds struck the sails, they had looked away a moment & looking again the boat was gone."

Tears prick at the corners of my eyes, a familiar feeling of helplessness and sadness brought on by her words. I lost my sister to cancer; I looked away for a moment, and she was gone. So yes, sometimes the insider's view cuts too close to the bone. And sometimes, it offers company, as when Mary Shelley writes, "surely the time will come when I shall be at peace & my brain & heart be no longer alive with unutterable anguish . . ."

Emily Dickinson, the nineteenth-century American poet who wrote of both the grave and the seductions of death, offers joy and good humor in her letters: "To live is so startling, it leaves but little room for other occupations." She throws out jokes with ease, as when writing to her "little cousins" Louise and Frances Norcross about a recent visit: "Louise left a tumbler of sweet-peas on the green room bureau. I am going to leave them there until they make pods and sow themselves in the upper-drawer, and then I guess they'll blossom about Thanksgiving time."

Ten years and many letters later, the humor remains, again in a letter to the cousins: "There is a tree in Mr. Sweetser's woods that shivers. I am afraid it is cold. I am going to make it a little coat. I must make several, because it is as tall as the barn, and [I will] put them on as the circus men stand on each other's shoulders."

I am surprised not only by her humor but by her willingness to engage with the outside world: I had always supposed Dickinson to be private and withdrawn, but her letters demonstrate another side to her character. Her correspondence with T. W. Higginson began after he published an article in the *Atlantic Monthly* in 1862 encouraging young writers. Dickinson sent him a sample of her writing, asking in the accompanying note, "Are you too deeply occupied to say if my verse is alive . . . Should you think it breathed, and had you the leisure to tell me, I should feel quick gratitude."

Higginson wrote back, encouraging her in her writing but dissuading her from seeking publication because of the very rare and strange form of her poetry; as he wrote later, he tried to "lead her in the direction of rules and traditions" and yet he admitted that it was her "unregenerate condition" that made her so interesting.

When he asked for a picture, Dickinson wrote back that she had not one photo of herself: "Could you believe me without? I had no portrait, now, but am small, like the wren; and my hair is bold, like the chestnut bur; and my eyes, like the sherry in the glass, that the guest leaves. Would this [description] do just as well?"

Dickinson's letters to Higginson are effusive and deliberate and lovely, as in the one in which she warns him against the dangers of going off to fight for the North in the Civil War: "I should have liked to see you before you became improbable . . . Should you, before this reaches you, experience Immortality, who will inform me of the exchange? Could you, with honor, avoid death, I entreat you sir."

Higginson made it through alive and after the war he finally came to visit Dickinson in Amherst. She expressed her gratitude in a letter: "The vein cannot thank the artery, but her solemn indebtedness to him, even the stolidest admit, and so of me who try, whose effort leaves no sound" and again months later, "Thank you for having been to Amherst. Could you come again that would be far better."

I love Dickinson best when she expresses her independence of mind, as in the letter in which she explains to Higginson her self-sufficiency, both material and spiritual: "When much in the woods, as a little girl, I was told that the snake would bite me, that I might pick a poisonous flower, or goblins would kidnap me; but I went along and met no one but angels, who were far shyer of me than I could be of them."

And I love her sense of humor and wonder.

Dickinson wrote to her cousins, "I open my window, and it fills the chamber with white dirt. I think God must be dusting." And later: "Spring is a happiness so beautiful, so unique, so unexpected, that I don't know what to do with my heart . . . Life is a spell so exquisite that everything conspires to break it."

Dickinson's exultation in spring's arrival matches my own—"The wind blows gay today and the jays bark like blue terriers"—and her devotion to her family a mirror for how I feel: "We are thinking most of Thanksgiving than anything else just now—how full will be the circle, less then by none—how the things will smoke—how the board will groan with the thousand savoury viands—how when the day is done, lo, the evening cometh, laden with merrie laugh and happy conversation . . . Thanksgiving indeed to a family united once more together."

I understand the thrill of writing unbounded—"I had no monarch in my life, and cannot rule myself; and when I try to organize, my little force explodes and leaves me bare and charred"—and I am pleased to see that, as I do, Dickinson found beauty and inspiration in the works of writers she loved, including Elizabeth Barrett Browning and George Eliot ("this mortal has already put on immortality"). For, as she writes in a letter to her dear cousins, "love, like literature, is exceeding great reward."

And how rewarded I am, to find in my new friend Emily her shared understanding of the importance of letters: "A letter is a joy of earth— it is denied the Gods."

"Dear Dad," begins the letter Hawkeye Pierce writes to his father during the first season of the TV show *M*A*S*H*. It is the day before Christmas and Hawkeye has been busy: "Hello at last, after almost three straight days of meatball surgery, seventy straight hours of sewing kids back together." Not the usual Christmas letter, but *M*A*S*H* was an unusual show. Based on the hit movie of the same name, the TV show ran for eleven seasons and was the single-most-watched TV show of my adolescence. I never missed it and when reruns began, I was right there.

M*A*S*H was a show about a United States military surgical unit doing its best to keep injured troops alive during the Korean War. Struggling for normalcy, the M*A*S*H crew keep themselves sane by playing football, preparing martinis, chasing sex, and attending monthly morality lectures conducted by their commanding officer. But the realities of war intrude daily. And the writers of the show often used letters as the device to describe such realities.

Hawkeye writes his Christmas letter home to his dad to explain what happened when he planned to play Santa Claus to a group of Korean children. He dressed up in cotton-ball mustache, beard, and brows and shoved ratty pillows under a nurse's red robe to add a belly roll to his war-shrunk frame. Fixing a red stocking cap on top of his head, Hawkeye Santa is all set to go out and entertain the kiddies.

But then a call comes in: a group of American soldiers is under heavy fire and a commander has been shot in the chest. Hawkeye, chest surgeon extraordinaire, is the only one who can help. He heads for the army helicopter, still dressed in his white beard, red cap, and bulging belly. Before leaving, he offers a quick good-bye to his friend Trapper McIntyre. Both men know he might not return from the mission.

Closing in on the field where the wounded commander and his soldiers cower under constant fire, Hawkeye scribbles out the last words to his dad, "I never thought I'd be flying in dressed as Kris Kringle but then those kids down there are in the last place they ever figured." Hawkeye signs off the letter and turns to the task at hand, dropping from the helicopter slowly, inching his way down a swinging rope.

Soldiers watch from below, transfixed. Their belief in Santa—and in the possibilities of the season—is rekindled by the vision of red-bellied Hawkeye, shimmying down to their rescue. And through his letter home, I—along with millions of other TV viewers—join in the faith.

My favorite "letter" episode is the one in which the M*A*S*H crew are suffering through seemingly interminable days of rain. In the midst of all the gloom and damp, a mail packet arrives. It's addressed to Hawkeye and comes from his hometown of Crabapple Cove, Maine. A high school friend of his is now a teacher in the town and the packet contains letters that her students have written. She writes to Hawkeye that the students prepared their letters in the hope of providing a little entertainment, "having heard how boring it is over there."

The letters are passed out among the main characters—BJ, Charles, Colonel Potter, Margaret, Father Mulcahy, and Hawkeye—with the admonition from Hawkeye that there will be no "stealing, selling, or swapping of letters" and that all letters must be responded to. But when he reads the letter he has been given, Hawkeye blanches at the task before him. A young boy has written that his oldest brother, Keith, was injured in Korea, fixed up by army doctors, and then returned to battle, where he was killed.

"You doctors just make people better so they can end up dead. I hate you all," writes Ronnie, the boy from Crabapple Cove. With those words, Ronnie explains in a nutshell the struggle Hawkeye has with his work every single day (and over the past nine seasons of M*A*S*H): why patch these kids up, if it is only to send them back to the front lines to kill or be killed?

Hawkeye tries to dodge the letter writing, explaining to Father Mulcahy that "I'm a large cog in the war machine . . . I'm in weapons repair . . . I can't deny doing it and I can't live with it." Yet Father Mulcahy urges him to write back to Ronnie and Hawkeye struggles on, trying to formulate an answer. When a young girl with a head injury is brought into the unit and Hawkeye becomes acutely aware of his ability to save her life, the advice he will offer Ronnie crystallizes.

Hawkeye begins his letter to Ronnie by warning him against hatred: "It's a shame to let the love you have for your brother turn to hate for others. Hate makes war, and war is what killed Keith. I understand how you feel. Sometimes I hate myself for being here." Then he goes on to explain that "once in a while in the midst of all this insanity, a very small event can make my being here almost bearable. I'm sorry I don't have an answer for you, Ronnie, except to suggest that you look for good wherever you can find it." Hawkeye's letter to Ronnie is an insider's view of war, a doctor's dose of understanding and acceptance, and of looking for something bright in the darkness.

The movie *Letters from Iwo Jima* begins with the scene of a leather satchel being dug up from the floor of a cave somewhere on the island of Iwo Jima. What is in the satchel? It is not until the movie ends and we see that same satchel first being buried that we know: the bag contains the letters written by Japanese soldiers stationed on the island of Iwo Jima in 1945.

The soldiers were doomed to fight a losing battle against the Americans in the final stages of World War II. Forced to wear a brave face in front of their commanders and fellow soldiers, the men can release their fears and say their final good-byes on paper: "Mother, I hope this money will help, as it is all I have left. I won't be needing anything from now on," writes one soldier, and even Baron Nishi, the brave and dashing officer of the Imperial Army, writes to his family with humble resignation: "Do not expect my return. In the end, I would just like to say, my heart has always been with you." The commanding officer, Kuribayashi, offers somber reflection in his letter to his son: "The life of your father is like a flicker of flame before the wind."

"We dig all day. We dig holes where we are able to stand when battle comes," writes the character Saigo in a heartbreaking scene. Conscripted into war and taken from his tiny village, Saigo is writing to his wife back home. "Holes just big enough to stand in. Not wide enough to move forward or back. Holes where we are expected to fight and stay in until we die . . . now I know what it feels like to dig my own grave."

But Saigo doesn't die and it is he who buries the letters of his compatriots, written but never delivered. He leaves them deep in the dirt floor of the cave, to be found decades later as artifacts of war.

Love-Letters Between a Nobleman and His Sister is a book that explores, entirely through letters, the forbidden love between a man and his sister-in-law: "What is it to my divine Sylvia, that the priest took my hand and gave it to your sister? What alliance can that create? Why should a trick devised by the wary old, only to make provision for posterity, tie me to eternal slavery?"

Penned by the Englishwoman Aphra Behn in 1684, *Love-Letters Between a Nobleman and His Sister* was not the first epistolary novel ever written. The genre's name comes from the Greek word *epistole* and the Old English *epistle,* meaning letter, and dates back to the 1400s, when the Spaniard Diego de San Pedro wrote his novel *Cárcel de Amor* (Prison of Love). By the late seventeenth century, the genre had taken off, with the French *Letters of a Portuguese Nun* by Gabriel-Joseph de Lavergne (although some argue it was written by a woman, Mariana Alcoforado), and the English novel *Familiar Letters*, written by James Howell. But it took Aphra Behn to make the epistolary novel a blockbuster.

Behn was best known for her plays, risqué and lively romps that pleased Charles II of England and led Alexander Pope to pen the words "The stage how loosely does Astrea tread / Who fairly puts all characters to bed." (Astrea was Aphra Behn's pen name.) Behn also wrote elegies, poems, travel memoirs, novels, and translations of works from French to English.

Born the daughter of a barber, Behn spent part of her childhood in Suriname and one of her most famous novels, *Oroonoko*, about a slave revolt, is based in part on her experiences there (and was the first English novel to demonstrate sympathy for the plight of slaves). After her father died, the family returned to England. While in her early twenties, Aphra met and married John Behn, a Dutchman by ethnicity. When he died a few years later, she was hired by the court of Charles II to become a spy in Antwerp, familiar as she was with the Dutch tongue.

Behn worked hard for Charles II, securing sources of information through all sorts of means (she took on a number of lovers in Antwerp) and providing tidbits of intelligence through secret letters sent back to the king from his "Astrea." Unfortunately, King Charles neglected to pay Behn for her hard work and she returned to England completely broke. She landed in debtors prison and was only released when an anonymous sponsor paid her bills. Now thirty years old, Behn used her freedom to forge a new life for herself, a life based on words. She wrote bawdy pieces caricaturing contemporary society and raising eyebrows right and left. She asserted for herself a freedom never before seen in women authors, boldly writing of love and sex, politics and class. Virginia Woolf proclaimed, more than three hundred and fifty years later, "All women together, ought to let flowers fall on the grave of Aphra Behn . . . for it was she who earned them the right to speak their minds."

But Behn was never so loose or so outspoken that her loyalty to king and country came into doubt. She was a devoted Royalist (despite the money owed her for her earlier services) and if she made fun of the social and sexual games of the aristocracy, she upheld the political ones. When she died in 1689, she was honored with burial in Westminster Abbey, the final resting place of many esteemed English writers, where her tombstone proclaims "Here lies a Proof that Wit can never be Defence enough against Mortality."

The tombstone lied: Behn did defend against mortality through the wit of her writings. She lives on through her wild novel *Love-Letters Between a Nobleman and His Sister.* The book is like one giant mash-up of all of Shakespeare's comedies: there are ill-fated lovers, disguised lovers, and mistaken-gender lovers; and there are letters, always the letters, falling into the wrong hands, or arriving too late into the right ones; the forged letters and the false letters, the true letters and the blue letters.

And the very, very purple letters: "I find a strange disorder in my blood, that pants and burns in every vein, and makes me blush, and sigh, and grow impatient, ashamed, and angry . . . I lay extended on my bed, undressed, unapprehensive of my fate, my bosom loose and easy of access, my garments thin and wantonly put on, as if they would with little force submit to the fond straying hand . . . I quite fainted in your arms, and left you triumphant lord of all."

What a raucous romp, to have Philander the husband fall in love with Sylvia, his sister-in-law. He runs off with her, then becomes bored with her, then rediscovers his passion for her. In the end, Philander runs off with the sister of Octavio, and Octavio becomes the lover of Sylvia, now that she has been jilted by Philander. Easy to follow? No, not at all. How amazing that the entire twisting and turning plot is achieved through the letters that the various characters write back and forth to each other! And it is through these letters that I find it so easy to understand the characters (if not the plot). After all, I was given full access to the hearts and minds of all the characters through their letters; a fly on the wall of their very lively chambers.

Sylvia keeps Octavio salivating while writing to Philander of her fears that he is cheating on her. Philander deflects the accusations of Sylvia by writing back, "Why all these doubts and fears? I fear this first reproaching me is rather the affects of your own guilt, it is the waves that roll and glide away, and not the steady shore."

Which of the two lovers is the shore, and which the waves? I know that both Philander and Sylvia roll with the punches of love, and neither is steady. I know, because I have read all the letters, and have seen, without restraint or censoring, how loyalties waver, lust lingers, vengeance boils, and hearts molder away: "For all my honour lost, my youth undone, my beauty tarnished . . . she that had the courage to abandon all for love and faithless thee, can, when she finds herself betrayed and lost, nobly revenge the ruin of her fame, and send thee to the other world."

The popularity of the epistolary novel has waxed and waned over the years, but as a genre it will always hold its own. *The Guernsey Literary and Potato Peel Pie Society* by Mary Ann Shaffer and Annie Barrows was the rage with book groups a few years back, and *The Perks of Being a Wallflower* by Stephen Chbosky was a recent hit with teens.

Griffin and Sabine by Nick Bantock is a novel that not only allows readers the insider's view provided by letters but the actual letter-opening experience. Contained within the pages of the novel are postcards and envelopes containing letters. The reader is invited to open the envelopes and read the letters, becoming not only a fly on the wall but a player in the drama of discovery. How can Sabine divine the thoughts of Griffin, half a world away? She attempts to reassure him, "I wonder if we will ever understand how and why we are linked. Griffin, why try? Let us simply take pleasure in each other." Fine advice, gleaned from my position as spy and participant.

Back in adolescence, about the same time I was watching *M*A*S*H* on television, I read *Daddy-Long-Legs* by Jean Webster. Then I read it again, and again. The novel is written as a series of letters sent from Judy Abbott, a young girl off at college, to the man ("Daddy-Long-Legs") who is providing the funding for her education, and I loved it for its very romantic representation of college life. The novel was written in 1912 (the same year James Seligman graduated from Princeton) and did not reflect college life in the 1970s, when I first read the book. But it wasn't reality, necessarily, that I was looking for. My mother, after all, was a professor at Northwestern University and as a kid growing up in a college town, I had a pretty good understanding of what went down at college.

But through the letters of the fictional Miss Judy Abbott, I escaped to a very beautiful and inspiring vision of college: "College is a very satisfying sort of life; the books and study and regular classes keep you alive mentally, and then when your mind gets tired, you have the gymnasium and outdoor athletics, and always plenty of congenial friends who are thinking about the same things you are. We spend a whole evening in nothing but talk—talk—talk—and go to bed with a very uplifted feeling, as though we had settled permanently some pressing world problems."

It helped that Judy was an avid reader like me: when she describes how she looks "forward all day to evening, and then I put an 'engaged' sign on the door and get into my nice red bath robe and furry slippers and pile all the cushions behind me on the couch, and light the brass student lamp at my elbow, and read and read and read," it is as if she is allowing me into paradise with her.

One of Peter's favorite books when he was a little boy was *Love, Your Bear Pete* by Dyan Sheldon. The book tells the story of a young girl, Brenda, who leaves her stuffed bear on the bus. Brenda's mom calls the bus depot, but no one has turned in a "small blue bear with one black eye, one green eye, and one and a half ears." Brenda is despondent. Her stuffed and loved companion, whom she has had with her every single day as far back as she can remember, is gone.

A week or so later, a postcard comes in the mail. It is a postcard from Pete. He is fine and well and visiting London: "London is very crowded but I'm lonely without you." More and more post-cards arrive, from Paris and Venice and Tangiers and Moscow and the Grand Canyon. Every postcard offers details of Pete's travels around the world: eating gelato, riding in a gondola and on a camel, visiting fruit markets, and sleeping out under the stars. And then one day, the postcards stop. Brenda is worried that Pete has forgotten about her until her mother hands her a package, wrapped in brown paper and addressed to Brenda. Inside, she finds her bear, Pete. He has come home after all his adventures away. I think what fascinated my Peter about the bear Pete was that a stuffed animal had a whole other side to him that Peter had never imagined before. Pete the bear had hidden desires—to travel and to experience the world—and all of a sudden, through the postcards he wrote, Peter was privy to the wanderlust of a previously homebound bear. Peter looked at his own stuffed bear with a new respect and admiration for what that little hunk of cloth and stuffing was capable of. He also clung that much more tightly to Teddy when we went out, for fear of losing his companion to the seductions of far-off travel!

When I left Peter on the steps of Memorial Hall at the start of his freshman year, I was tempted to cling as tightly to him then as he had held on to Teddy at age three. But what I can discover about him now that he is away—through his letters home—just might be recompense for his absence. I will know him in a new way, as the man he is becoming and the very distinct being he has always been growing into. I will be granted continual revelation of my son through the wedge of space he allocates for me, the insider view he allows onto his everyday, faraway life.

7

Tender Offering

For his heart was in his work, and the heart
giveth grace unto every Art.
> —Henry Wadsworth Longfellow,
> *"The Building of the Ship"*

Early in the evening of February 20, 1862,
Willie Lincoln died of typhoid fever,
contracted from drinking water piped into the
White House from the Potomac River. He was
eleven years old. The Lincolns were devastated.
The president staggered from his son's deathbed,
crying out, "My poor boy. He was too good for
this earth . . . I know that he is much better off in
heaven, but then we loved him so. It is hard, hard
to have him die!"

Willie was his mother's favorite child, his
younger brother Tad's hero, and his father's
companion. Visitors to the White House often
saw Willie and his father walking together
through the halls, hand in hand and chatting away.

The funeral for William Wallace Lincoln was
held at the White House four days after he died.

Horrendous storms hit Washington that day, thunder rattling the windows of the White House. Willie was laid out in a coffin in the Green Room, dressed in simple pants and a black jacket, a white shirt and white stockings. He held a small bouquet of flowers. The flowers would later be given to his mother, who remained upstairs the entire day, weeping.

Letters of condolence arrived at the White House, words of sympathy offered to ease the family's pain. George McClellan was one of Lincoln's generals, but the two men did not like or trust each other. Nevertheless, McClellan put aside all animosity in writing to Lincoln, sending only his compassion for the grieving family: "I cannot refrain from expressing to you the sincere and deep sympathy I feel for you. . . . I wish now only to assure you and your family that I have felt the deepest sympathy in your affliction."

"I was surprised about the announcement of the death of your son Willie. I thought him a smart boy for his age, so considerate, so manly, his knowledge and good sense far exceeding most boys more advanced in years," wrote William Florville, a black barber from Illinois who had known the Lincoln family in their Springfield days. "Yet the time comes to all, all must die."

Former president Franklin Pierce wrote what words of consolation he could: "In this hour, so full of danger to our country, and of trial and anxiety to all good men . . . your own cherished boy . . . will nestle in your heart until you meet him in that new life, where tears and toils and conflict will be unknown."

Pierce had lost three children, including his eleven-year-old son, Benny. In 1853, on the way to Washington, DC, to begin his presidency, the train on which he and his family were traveling broke an axle and went over an embankment. Pierce and his wife were thrown from the car, but when they turned back to look for Benny, they saw his body crushed and then his head severed by the force of the falling train.

Mrs. Pierce never recovered from the shock. She spent her years at the White House composing notes and letters to Benny and to another son, Frank, who had died at age four from typhus, and pretending to play with her first baby, Franklin Jr., who died at just three days old. When Pierce wrote to Lincoln "your great domestic affliction . . . brought back the crushing sorrow," his words were weighted with his own deep awareness of the anguish in mourning the loss of a child.

Later that same year, Lincoln would write a letter of condolence after his good friend William McCullough died fighting for the Union in Mississippi. Lincoln feared for the health of McCullough's daughter, Fanny: "It is with deep regret that I learn of the death of your kind and brave father, and especially that it is affecting your young heart beyond what is common in such cases . . . You cannot now realize that you will ever feel better . . . You are sure to be happy again. To know this, which is certainly true, will make you some less miserable now. I have had experience enough to know what I say, and you need only to believe it to feel better at once. The memory of your dear father, instead of an agony, will yet be a sad, sweet feeling in your heart, of a purer and holier sort than you have known before."

In November 1864, Lincoln wrote his most famous letter of condolence to Mrs. Bixby of Massachusetts. Lincoln had been told that she was the mother of five sons, all of whom had died fighting for the Union cause. Later information would prove that in fact two of her five children had been killed in the war and it was possible that two others had actually deserted the Union cause. But none of that mattered, then or now. A mother had lost her children.

Lincoln expressed his own hard-earned understanding of "how weak and fruitless must be any word of mine which should attempt to beguile you from the grief of a loss so overwhelming." Then he went on: "I cannot refrain from tendering you the consolation that may be found in the thanks of the Republic . . . I pray that our Heavenly Father may assuage the anguish of your bereavement, and leave you only the cherished memory of the loved and lost."

"I have shed many, many tears . . . If it were not for the hope that by serving God rightly here we might be able to meet them again, what would life be?" wrote Mary Todd Lincoln to the husband of Willie's teacher, Hester Reeves, when Reeves died just weeks after Willie. "Please excuse this letter written in much haste and almost blotted by my tears. When we weep here, we can only remember that, there, all tears are wiped away from their eyes. Sorrow never enters there."

Mary Todd Lincoln offered compassion through her tears, the soaked letter underscoring her empathy. A letter written in grief has the power to assuage grief, both for the writer and for the recipient. There can be no greater kindness, no greater offering of compassion, than the lessening of sorrow and the bringing of comfort through a letter.

Maude Fisher, a Red Cross worker serving in France in World War I, cared for a young American soldier named Richard Hogan. Hogan had fallen victim to the flu epidemic that swept through Europe and across America, killing over 50 million people. Fisher wrote to tell his family the sad news of his death, sending her letter from the small village of Commercy to the soldier's family home in Massachusetts.

Fisher began the letter with the facts of Hogan's disease and death: "He was brave and cheerful . . .

and made a good fight with the disease . . . Everything was done to make him comfortable and I think he suffered very little, if any pain."

She described his final resting place, where he "sleeps under a simple white wooden cross among his comrades . . . I enclose here a few leaves from the grass that grows near in a pretty meadow. A big hill overshadows the place and the sun was setting behind it just as the Chaplain said the last prayer over your boy . . . From the whole hospital force, accept deepest sympathy and from myself, tenderest love in your hour of sorrow."

If my son were sent far away and became ill or was injured in battle, I would want to know that someone held his hand at the end, stroked his cheek, and listened to his last words. I would want to know that he was buried in a place with grass, dappled sun, and at least a promise of peace. A letter written to me assuring me of such final care for my child would not take away my grief but its words would offer some soothing of my pain.

Thomas Merton, the Trappist monk and poet, wrote a letter of condolence to the father of one of the children killed in the September 1963 bombing of a Baptist church in Birmingham, Alabama. Denise McNair and three of her classmates died in their Sunday school classroom, blown apart by a bomb. As Merton wrote to the father, Chris McNair, "There is so much to say, and there are no words with which to say it."

Merton wrote that Denise "remains as a witness to innocence and to love, and inspiration to all of us who remain to face the labor, the difficulty, and the heart-break of the struggle for human rights and dignity." It is the fate—and the grace—of humans, that we reach out, even, as Merton described himself, as "a total stranger," to offer the promise of "mercy and goodness" and of remembrance; that those who have died will never be "forgotten on earth."

I know from my own experience what a tender letter can do. After my sister died, I heard from many people, some of whom had never met Anne-Marie but knew me well, as well as from a number of her friends, a few of whom I had never met. Teachers from the local schools wrote to me, and coworkers from offices I had left long ago. After publishing a book about my sister's death and my struggle to deal with sorrow, people from all over the world wrote to me, telling me of their own losses and sorrows, and offering condolences for my own. All the letters I received offered wishes that I would feel better, and promises that my sister would be remembered, in prayers and memories or conversations.

Remembrance was found in the letters them-selves. In words, sent to me across miles or countries or oceans, handwritten on cards and lined paper and ivory stationery. An old friend of Anne-Marie wrote of how my sister defined "cool" with her strong sense of self and unruffled demeanor: "The rest of us would be freaking out about something and Anne-Marie would just smile the cat-smile, and we would all calm down." I knew that smile well. The letter of her friend helps me to see it again.

Another friend sent copies of poems Anne-Marie had written in high school, and wrote that my sister's works, written at such a young age, expressed a deep understanding of the exigencies of living: "and I hope you can draw from her words . . . the resources to continue living, as she did, in exacting wonder of the world." How powerful this sentence was for me at that time and today, almost a decade later. I have the words my sister wrote, and I have the bundles of letters written about her after she died, each offering me consolation.

Hundreds of condolence letters poured in to Jeanne Ashe and her six-year-old daughter, Camera, after her husband, Arthur Ashe, died in February 1993. Ashe was forty-nine years old when he died of AIDS-related illness, having contracted AIDS after receiving a blood trans-fusion following heart surgery. Long famous as an international tennis star and a leader in the fight against discrimination and segregation, Ashe had become a spokesman about AIDS in the final years of his life, and a proponent for more research, understanding, and sympathy for people living with the disease.

One of the condolence letters that came to the Ashe family seemed at first to be a simple offering of condolences. But on the second page of the letter, the writer reveals the fact of his HIV-positive status. It is a secret he has kept from all but a few friends. He writes about how he met Ashe once at a special event and still remembers his calm demeanor and his kindness. Unsure now of his own future, the letter writer finds strength in how Ashe had lived with AIDS. With his carefully folded sheets of lined paper, he sought to share that strength, needed now by the family Ashe left behind.

Many of the letters sent to the Ashe family offered a personal anecdote to illustrate the magic of Ashe's personality. A man who once traveled with Ashe on a plane recounts how suddenly the plane began to pitch and dive; the traveler was certain it would crash. But then he looked over to see Ashe flipping through a magazine, unconcerned and cool as a cucumber. He knew then that the plane would make it safely to their destination and "we would all be alright."

One family wrote about the time Ashe spoke at the commencement ceremonies conducted by Harvard Medical School; Ashe had been "the first one to call our son doctor. I shall always remember that. I shall never forget Arthur Ashe." An older white woman wrote that watching Ashe conduct himself through years as a tennis star and then sports commentator had forced her to confront her prejudices: "He helped a lot of us to overcome the prejudice buried within."

A personal story offers enduring consolation: a shared memory or some new aspect of the person now revealed through an anecdote. When President John F. Kennedy was assassinated, letters of condolence flooded the White House, hundreds of thousands from around the world. Many of the writers offered remembrances of seeing Kennedy on the campaign trail, how they waited in the cold or the rain or the heat, and then the wonderful moment when he appeared: "His eyes were sparkling, a grin as wide as his face. It was such a warm smile. Oh, how lucky you were to see it so often."

Another writes about how Kennedy lifted her baby up in the air, then "took the time to tell me what a beautiful baby she was, and how much she resembled her mother." Another writes of how she invited President Kennedy to her house for coffee: "I had no bone to pick, I was only writing for friendship." President Kennedy couldn't make it to her place for coffee, but Mrs. Kennedy's secretary sent a note thanking her for the offered kindness. "I was so very happy to get that answer."

Sympathy is also offered by extending a wish for an easing of pain and the granting of peace. In a note to Jeanne and Camera Ashe, an old acquaintance promises that "in time the darkness will wear off" and another offers the wish, "May you find peace in the fact that you gave so much love to this dear person."

A group of schoolchildren sent in their crayon wishes for "rainbows" to shower down on Jeanne and Camera, and one sweet child added to Camera, "I hope your father has a good time in heaven." Another underscored how sorry she felt by trying to explain how she, too, understood pain: "I am very very very very very sorry and sad that your father died. I broke my arm." More than a few of the letters written by the schoolchildren offered the simple words "I love you."

My son George had a friend who died the summer before their eighth-grade year. Tess was on a camp trip in Maine when the van she was traveling in was struck from behind by a tractor-trailer carrying sawdust down from the pine mills. In the days that followed her death, our town gathered around Tess's mother and brother, giving what support we could in the form of meals, hugs, or simply the presence of another person, a sheltering arm across caved shoulders and an abiding witness to the sudden and horrible void caused by the death of a child.

Tess's friends wanted to do something substantial for Tess's family. It was one of her closest friends who came up with the idea of letters.

Vignesh asked each of her friends to write a letter, expressing exactly what Tess had meant to him or her. George wrote about how he was always a little envious of Tess: "that drive, that ambition . . . The world is turning, Tess, but you are lost, and that makes the whole rotation different." Remembering her is part of the new rotation, and as constant as its insistent roll: "I miss you."

The letters were gathered in a notebook and given to Tess's mother. Suzanne keeps those letters close and reads through them often. The letters of condolence will offer lasting consolation: memories of Tess, created by her childhood friends, bringing sympathy and a moment of grace.

I know a woman who writes letters to her "dear sister who passed away three years ago" and to her mother, who died recently. "It's been part of the grieving and healing process, and a spiritual connection to them" she told me. In her letters, she shares everything going on in her life, in the world, and with other family members: "It is my journey and journal of life here on this good earth. I love the thought that they are the angels on my shoulders."

Writing a letter of condolence is an example of the two-way street of altruism, where in the giving there is as much benefit as in the receiving. I know that for my son George, to write a letter to Tess telling her how he would always remember her and have her with him in his memories was as much a consolation for himself. It allowed an acceptance of pain, a promise of remembrance, and an avowal of living. It became okay for my son to live on while his friend had died, because he had promised to remember her in his living. And he will keep that promise, in part because of the letter he wrote.

Most ancient Egyptians could neither read nor write, but they did send letters. Professional scribes offered writing and reading services for a price, and for those unable to afford the pros, educated friends and relatives were imposed upon, again and again. Thousands of letters have been discovered in the past century or so, covering almost all the periods of Egyptian kingdoms over millennia of time.

The importance of letters in ancient Egypt can be seen in the advice sent by a professional scribe to his young apprentice: "[Apply yourself to this] noble profession . . . You will find it useful . . . Love writing, shun dancing; then you become a worthy official . . . Befriend the scroll, the palette. It pleases more than wine. Writing for him who knows it is better than all other professions. It pleases more than bread and beer, more than clothing and ointment. It is worth more than an inheritance in Egypt, than a tomb in the west."

"It is good if the Lord . . . takes note" is the

recurring refrain in many of the letters I've read from ancient Egypt. Who was this "Lord" that is advised to take note? He was the overseer of the local temple, something like the mayor in a present-day city hall. The overseer took charge of the grains and other goods that were delivered to the temple (like our property tax) and then redistributed to the surrounding communities. Requests of all kinds came into the overseer, asking for everything from linen for weavers "left abandoned . . . and unable to weave clothes" to "grain provisions and the confections for the daily offerings," and from "some natron" (used in embalming) to "some raisins for me, your humble servant."

The requests were forthright in what was needed—no beating around the bush for the ancient Egyptians—and then finished off with a final flourish of thanks for anticipated fulfillment of those needs: "It is good if the Lord, l.p.h., takes note" (l.p.h. being the obligatory blessing of "life, prosperity, and health"). These "It is good" letters were thank-you notes written in anticipation of favors granted: "This is a communication to the Lord, l.p.h., about sending some milk for me, your humble servant. It is good if you take note."

The living received thanks in ancient Egypt, but the dead got guilt-trip letters along the lines of "I did so much for you when you were alive and this is the thanks I get?" These letters detail what was done for the dead person in life, and now demand what is due back from the after-world. One poor dead wife is harassed by her living husband for failing to ameliorate some lingering illness of his: "Since I am your beloved on earth, fight on my behalf and intercede on behalf of my name. I did not garble a spell in your presence when I perpetuated your name on earth. Remove the infirmity from my body!"

And a son writes to his mother, "I, your son, then brought you seven quails and you ate them. Is it in your presence that I am being injured so that my children are disgruntled and I, your son, am ill?" In the age before aspirin and antibiotics, intervention from the great beyond was deemed necessary—and a debt come due, in return for all the good done on behalf of the dead person in life.

A man writes to his deceased wife: "What have I done against you wrongfully for you to get into this evil disposition in which you are? . . . I took you for a wife when I was a youth . . . I did not divorce you . . . when you became ill with the disease you contracted, I sent for a chief physician, and he treated you and did what you told him to do . . . I donated clothing of fine linen to wrap you up in . . . I overlooked nothing good so as not to have it done for you . . . I've spent these last three years without entering another house . . . as for those sisters in the household, I have not entered into a one of them." And, yes, he *does* mean physically enter into them.

So what does he get for his loyalty when she was alive and chastity now that she is dead? Apparently, not enough: "I shall litigate with you and right shall be distinguished from wrong." I wonder if there were law firms which specialized in suits against the badly behaving dead in ancient Egypt. I can imagine the billboards: "Wronged by the dead? We bring final judgment for you to enjoy." But maybe all the husband wanted was a simple thank-you, a token of appreciation channeled through to him now as a bit of good luck on earth.

Sigmund Freud sent appreciation to a friend through a thank-you note in 1887, when he wrote expressing gratitude for both the "cordial letter" and the "magnificent gift," which "awakened the most pleasant memories for me" of Christmases past and now offered great hope for the future: the enjoyment of "a lively and mutually gratifying relationship between the two of us." Raymond Chandler, the writer of dark detective stories and a notorious hard-ass, was less effusive but just as sincere in his thank-you notes: "Thank you for yours of July 12 [a letter] and for taking the trouble to cover so much paper at a time when you had a stiff wrist."

The thank-you, like the condolence letter, is a two-way street. It is a form of acknowledgment that I trace to the Egyptians and their "It is good" phraseology, and a genre of letter I have found in virtually every collection of correspondence that I have ever read. In the hundreds of volumes of letters I've read over my lifetime, the most commonly expressed emotion is not love or consolation but thanks.

In 1921, Mrs. W. C. Lathrop of Norton, Kansas, wrote to Thomas Edison to thank him for making electricity a part of her daily life. She begins, "It is not always the privilege of a woman to thank personally the inventor of an article which makes life liveable for her sex." And then she counts the ways in which Edison has brought her pleasure, from the sound of her "wash machine chugging along" to being able to whip up meals on the electric range, from ironing clothes using "an electric mangle and with an electric iron" to cleaning her house with electric cleaners.

After all the housework is done, other rewards begin for Mrs. Lathrop, thanks to Mr. Edison. She restores herself using an electric massage, then curls her hair using an electric iron and dresses up "in a gown sewed on a machine run by a motor." Primped up and with time to relax, Mrs. Lathrop relies upon her electrically powered Victrola to "study Spanish for awhile or listen to . . . heavenly strains" of music, "forgetting I'm living in a tiny town of two thousand where nothing much ever happens."

What public figure would I write such a letter to? When I was eleven, I wrote to Dr Pepper to thank him for making such a great soda pop. It was with great surprise that I received a letter back from someone I'd never heard of (apparently there is no one named Pepper, doctor or otherwise) along with a cache of posters featuring Dr Pepper cans in enticing but strange circumstances—cruising on a motorcycle, surfside at the beach, on top of a mountain somewhere, snowcapped summits all around. I hung one poster in my locker at school and shelved the rest.

Most of my thank-you letters have been directed at people I know, people who actually do exist and have had an impact on my life in more ways than just providing an overly sweetened carbonated chemical concoction. My birthday cards to friends always thank them for their friendship, letters to Jack offer gratitude for his unwavering presence, notes to my children are about all the joy they've brought to my life.

The author E. M. Forster wrote, "There's enough sorrow in the world, isn't there, without trying to invent it." A corollary to that sentiment is that there is more than enough kindness in the world, isn't there: we just have to acknowledge it. And what better way than through a letter.

My friend Nancy recently shared with me the letters of her great-great-grandmother who was born in Missouri in the mid-1800s. Anna Eliza was married twice, inheriting a fortune from her first husband (which her second husband squandered on bad deals and gambling) and raising six children (three of whom would die during Anna Eliza's lifetime) through high times and hard times.

Anna Eliza wrote a vast number of letters, long and intimate, to George Smith. George was the son of David Smith, a free black man who seems to have worked as manager on the farms owned by Anna Eliza's first husband. David Smith also ran his own successful wagon business, taking advantage of the westward migration of the mid-1800s. Made wealthy by wagons, he used his profits to purchase slaves put up on the auction block and in danger of being separated from their families. He freed the purchased women and children and allowed the men to work for him to pay their own price out of bondage.

Anna Eliza met George, David's son, when he was five years old. George became a favorite of hers and the two spent a good deal of time together. His obituary states that she was like a mother to him, as his own mother died when he was just a few months old. George attended Oberlin College in the early 1870s and lost touch with Anna Eliza. After college, he went to work in Washington, DC, including a long tenure with Blanche K. Bruce, the only black Congressman to serve a full term until the 1960s (he served in the Senate from 1875 to 1881). Senator Bruce went on to become register of the treasury, and George Smith went with him.

It was in Washington, DC, that George renewed his friendship with Anna Eliza, having discovered that she was living for a brief time in the District. He wrote to her there, and a correspondence began. Although they did see each other occasionally (when Anna Eliza came to visit her daughters in DC), most of their adult friendship was through letters.

The expression of gratitude runs through the letters sent by Anna Eliza: gratitude for George's kindnesses and attention. She thanks him for his "most welcome letter"—"if it hadn't been that your cheery encouraging letter came . . . I would have had a hysteric [*sic*]"—and then apologizes for not having written back more promptly: "I suppose you have placed me on the list of those lost at sea in some late accident and imagine me forming the true inwardness of some epicurean shark!" or, "I guess the ink is blushing because I've neglected my favorite correspondent for so long!" She offers excuses for why she hasn't written back more promptly: "I found my time so full of children and the housekeeping that I hardly had time to say my prayers."

George is almost like a therapist, the man to whom she writes of secrets he must tell no one and to whom she complains openly about family and friends, cautioning him occasionally to keep her shared thoughts between them but knowing no such warning is necessary: "I'm talking very plainly but I know that I'm talking to a friend." She could not speak so freely if she were to meet face-to-face, and regularly, with George. It is the distance between them that allows her the space to write fully—and for that she is thankful: "May God bless you for your disinterested noble kindness."

Letters between me and my high school friends during our first years away at college functioned in much the same way. We could complain about classes, roommates, boys (to men), and lack of funds, as we could not when writing to our parents. And with new friendships forming, especially during freshman year, my true feelings about what was going on around me were kept tamped down. With the world always shifting, it was better to share the worst with old friends far away than with new acquaintances whom I could not quite rely on for discretion or honesty or compassion. I was happy to see envelopes waiting for me in my mail slot. It was unalloyed relief to be able to spill my guts in the letters I sent.

Gushing sentences of thanks always began our correspondence back and forth—"Thanks for the letter—I just got it!"—and ended the long hand-written notes as well: "Thanks again for always being there for me. I wish we were closer but at least we can write to each other." This was from Amy, a girl I'd known since kindergarten. Amy wasn't happy at school; one of her best friends had died over the summer and the heavy partying and huge population of strangers at the state university were not what she wanted or needed.

When I got the news that Amy was leaving college and going home, I understood that she wanted some space and peace to figure out her next step. I understood because we had shared our anxieties and our excitement—for me, the excitement of new classes and friends and unchaperoned freedom outweighed the anxieties such classes and friends and freedom brought. For Amy, the anxiety was too much. "But thank you for all the letters," she wrote. "They meant a lot." As did hers to me. We had shared thanks across time, and kindness always. As the ancient Egyptians would have said, it is good to take note.

8

Living Between Letters

Yet all experience is an arch wherethro'
Gleams that untravell'd world whose
    margin fades
For ever and for ever when I move.
    —Alfred, Lord Tennyson, *"Ulysses"*

For years, the only contact my father had with his family was through letters. He'd left his village in Belarus when he was eighteen, fleeing waves of military occupation during World War II: first the Germans and the Russians, then the Germans moving east, and then the Russians again moving west. Back and forth went control over Belarus, and farther away fled my father. Would he have left if he had known it would be fifty years before he saw his village again? Leaving might have saved his life, but it took him away from family.

My father found out about the murders of two of his brothers and a sister by letter, and it was a letter that later told him how another sister and his parents had left their village, running for their lives after the Soviet army invaded from the East. When the war ended, it was a letter delivered through the efforts of the Red Cross that informed my father of the deportation of his parents and sister from Germany back to Belarus.

My father escaped deportation by working as a cook for the American army. As the Iron Curtain descended, communication with his family was effectively cut off. When he began as a student at the University of Regensburg, his desire to share the good news with his parents was stifled. He was the first and only of his ten siblings to attend university and the news could have brought some joy to his parents, leavening their hardships in Soviet-controlled Belarus. But only his brother George, also working for the American army, could join in his celebration.

Through a program sponsoring refugees from Eastern Europe, my father eventually left Germany for Belgium to study at the University of Louvain. Just weeks after his arrival at university, a required medical exam revealed that he was suffering from tuberculosis. He was sent off again, this time to a sanatorium in Eupen, a small town set in the eastern hills of Belgium.

He lived in the sanatorium for two years, two months, and two days. Although friends visited from the university, no family came. George couldn't leave his post with the American army and the rest were behind the Iron Curtain. And then my father remembered that one of his mother's brothers might be close enough to come visit. Uncle Clement had joined the French Foreign Legion during World War I after escaping from a Polish concentration camp. Having served with the Foreign Legion all over the world, Uncle Clement had settled down somewhere in France. My father eagerly wrote to the French consulate, asking for help in locating Clement Shostakovich.

In a few weeks, a reply came. Uncle Clement lived on the Côte d'Azur, in a village called Châteauneuf de Grasse. My father wrote to him there and five weeks later, Uncle Clement arrived at the sanatorium in Eupen. Through a series of letters, my father's wish had come true: he was visited by family.

Uncle Clement stayed for a few days, coming every morning to sit beside my father and tell him anecdotes about the family, and about his own adventures in the French Foreign Legion. He told my father how he met the love of his life in Marrakesh, on an evening when he was out at a nightclub to see the cancan dancers. One particular dancer caught his eye. Her name was Ludmila, she was from Czechoslovakia, and within days she agreed to be his wife.

After a few days in Eupen visiting with my father, Uncle Clement returned home to his Ludmila. He left my father with a gold Napoleon coin and the promise to write soon.

Uncle Clement kept good on his promise, sending regular letters. With each letter, Uncle enclosed five hundred French francs, spare change to keep my father in frites and beer. That extra money was especially important once my father was finally released from the sanatorium and allowed to return to school in Louvain. He met my mother, a fellow student, in one of his philosophy classes. The lecture class on Saint Thomas Aquinas was not quite a nightclub in Marrakesh, but their romance flourished, fed by frites (funded by Clement), Ping-Pong, and conversation.

The letters between Uncle Clement and my father continued for years. My father wrote to Uncle Clement, filling him in on the news of his courtship of my mother, their marriage (Clement and Ludmila attended the wedding, dressed to the nines), the move to the United States, and, of course, the growing population of the American family (the births of me and my sisters). Letters to my father from Uncle Clement veered between life in his small village, with gossip about some of the more lively characters in his neighborhood, and news he'd received from family back in Belarus.

I first met Uncle and Aunt, as we called them, in the early 1970s. My family flew from Chicago to Paris, rented a car, and then drove south to their whitewashed village by the sea. I remember driving through fields of lavender, growing in acres after acres of hillsides. In the distance we could see splashes of red and orange against white; these were the flowers of geraniums, growing from pots on every balcony of Uncle and Aunt's village. The village itself was tiny, just an escalation of small houses along rows of narrow, winding streets.

We visited Uncle and Aunt two or three more times over the following summers. We took our rented car through fields of purple, all the time looking out for the geraniums, and Aunt's wildly waving arm, welcoming us back. During the hours we spent together, the adults shared stories and photo albums and memories. They drank wine from short glasses and laughed in loud bursts, while we kids sipped syrupy Coke from bottles and tried to understand the quickly flying French.

We went on excursions all over the countryside, with Aunt packed in alongside us girls in the backseat of the car and Uncle wedged in front next to my parents. One day we went to the beach in Nice, and coming back, we found ourselves stuck in what seemed like the longest traffic jam in history. An accident had stopped traffic going both ways on the narrow road that wound up from the sea, and all the travelers came out of their cars and set up impromptu picnics. Aunt still had food from our lunch, cheese and fruit and sausage, and we set ourselves up on a blanket, with a view all the way back down to the water.

The visits always came to an end, and we had to return to the United States and school, chores and work (and winter snow). What never ended, however, were the letters my father and Uncle Clement wrote. In the 1960s, letters had also started to come from family in the Soviet Union: his brothers, sister, and parents sent news, photos, and questions about our life in the United States.

The letters my father exchanged with Uncle, his parents, and siblings were his only connection with them. Other than the summer trips to France and visits with his brother George, those letters constituted the relationship he had with his family. But it was a relationship in bursts: information was shared through mail that could take anywhere from one week to two months to arrive.

What happened in the time between letters sent off and letters received? My father expected a response to the letters he wrote but he knew that the answers back would not come soon. There is something wonderful about that interval, the space between sending off a message and getting one back again. I like the idea of committing myself to paper, releasing those words to the intended recipient, and not waiting with held breath for a response, or checking every ten minutes for an update in status or incoming mail or text message. Instead, the letter is written and sent, and I continue on with my life. As my father continued on with his.

• • •

During World War I the Knights of Columbus arranged for special postcards to be provided to American soldiers waiting to be sent abroad. A soldier would sign his card beneath the prominently placed sentence I HAVE ARRIVED SAFELY OVERSEAS. In small letters at the bottom of the card was the promise *This card will be held until safe arrival of the boat on which I sailed.*

My friend Catherine's grandfather was given such a postcard. With careful script he wrote out his name—E. R. Lucht—to ensure that the good news of his safe arrival would be sent to his family back home. Catherine's family keeps that card safe to this day, as a guarantee and a talisman. Mechanic E. R. Lucht did make it overseas and back again, surviving the war to come home safe.

While he was overseas, Lucht wrote letters home to his parents filled with news about food and mud and new friends: "We are sleeping upstairs in one of these houses in this burg. We have everything in this building, sheep, cats, rabbits and dogs. We have more company here tonight, the old dog has some young puppies and believe me they sure make some noise too. The people here have about a couple hundred sheep."

With nothing about war or danger or fear, the letters were meant to reassure his family. The letters probably helped him as well, in tamping down fear and reasserting normalcy: "In spite of all the rain the fellows played football yesterday. The score was seven to seven so we didn't get beat and didn't lose neither. We have a good team and will play again pretty soon."

Weeks went by between letters written in France and those sent from back home. Lucht's were filled with details of easy living ("The gardens are fine over here and everything looks good . . . You should see all the grapes they grow over here, everywhere you look you can see large vineyards . . . I like this country") and about how he was mucking it out on his own as best he could.

The letters from home to Lucht were about everyday events (get-togethers and gossip) and came with enclosed photos of friends and family. "Don't forget to send some of you and Dad," Lucht reminded his parents. Letters back and forth, photos of smiling faces, and the time in between mail deliveries to breathe and to hope.

When I write a letter, I send it out and then go back to my day, my work and my children, the cats and Jack, books and food. Yes, I am waiting for an answer to my letter but waiting is not my main activity. To be dependent on e-mail and text is to have access to immediate response—but diminishes the rich opportunities that come from living with delayed gratification. For so much happens in the delay.

My father learned to speak French and play chess in the intervals between letters; he met my mother, finished medical school, and moved to a new country. It was in the time between letters written and letters received that my father learned to bear his sorrows and celebrate his joys, to experience life. With the press of technology, do we allow ourselves space to experience and become? Or have we fallen victim to the expectation of instant response? When tied to the gratification of digital communication, we can find ourselves only in the act of expecting, and not in the act of experiencing.

Jimmy Cliff, the Jamaican musician, wrote a song about waiting: "Sitting here in limbo, waiting for the tide to flow . . ." Waiting in limbo, waiting for the tide to flow, is when things happen. If we can only be there to notice the happening.

A written letter allows me both to notice the happening and to record it. To understand it perhaps a bit more by writing about it, and then to pass on what I've noticed through my writing. And after I've written my letter and sent it out, I can sit back and let the tide flow or I can run around while the tide flows, but no matter what, flow it will, giving me more to write about.

Rachel Carson, whose book *Silent Spring* was the catalyst for the environmental movement in the 1960s, exchanged hundreds of letters with her friend and the love of her life, Dorothy Freeman. She and Freeman had met back in the

1950s. It was a relationship started by a letter. In the fall of 1952 Carson purchased land on the coast of Maine to fulfill a lifelong dream of owning a house on the water. Freeman owned a summerhouse just down the road on the island of Southport and, having heard who her new neighbor would be, she sent Carson a welcoming letter. Carson wrote back—"What a charming and thoughtful greeting from our Southport neighbors!"—and their correspondence began.

The two women met in person during the summer of 1953. They took a walk together through the tidal pools of Southport Island at low tide, the stones and creatures and filtered sand as fascinating to one woman as to the other. From the start, the women understood they were soul mates, as Carson wrote to Freeman just weeks later: "It seems as though I had known you for years instead of weeks, for time doesn't matter when two people think and feel the same way about so many things."

When summer turned to fall and Carson returned to her home outside Washington, DC, and Freeman to West Bridgewater, Massachusetts, they wrote letters back and forth. Early on, their mutual love was acknowledged: Carson wrote to Freeman that it was their "kindred spirits" that lay "at the heart of our love." And as the months passed, love flourished; as Carson wrote to Freeman, "the necessity of writing instead of speaking, have contributed to the depth of love and understanding that have developed."

Letters carried the women through the winter, and in summer they were together again. In fall they separated but stayed close through their letters. Carson wrote to Freeman, "I didn't know then that you would claim my heart—that I would freely give you a lifetime's love and devotion . . . Now I know, and you know. And as I have given, I have received—the most precious of all gifts. Thank you, darling, with all my heart . . . some of our mystery is beyond comprehension, even as it sheds its radiant beauty on our lives."

Because the women became intimate friends so quickly, and yet maintained family-wide friendships as well, they often wrote two letters at a time to each other, one to be shared with family members, and the other meant just for one to the other. They called their private letters "apples," the word chosen because of a toy popular at the time, a wooden apple that could open at the top to reveal a smaller apple contained inside.

Carson and Freeman waited anxiously for each new apple. "Friday, I found myself watching for the mailman . . . although I told myself firmly that of course there wouldn't be anything from you—there just wouldn't! But the irresponsible half of me answered back that there just *might* be, and kept watching. And was so, so rewarded when there was your dear handwriting after all," Carson wrote, and Freeman wrote back, "I had talked to myself all morning to prepare myself for the fact that your letter couldn't possibly be in the mail today. But it was! How lovely."

Carson quickly saw the need to regulate their post, for fear of losing herself entirely to waiting anxiously each day for the mailman to come by. She had family to take care of, books to write, nature to observe, and, in the final years of their friendship, terrible health problems to deal with.

And so early on in their relationship, Carson devised a plan that the two should write each other just one letter a week: "I really believe the weekly schedule is best. It cuts down that 'waiting for the mailman' and I never quite settle down to work while I'm looking or listening for him. So far as that expected letter is concerned I think one a week is best."

Nevertheless, Carson was quick to add, "That doesn't mean darling, that I wouldn't welcome with joy a little unheralded one now and then, if you feel like writing it."

And later, she wrote again of the dilemma of wanting letters but needing the time spaced between them: "Darling—*did* I ask you for a letter every day? I didn't mean to, although of course I'd love it. But I know we shouldn't make that our routine, for many reasons. *So,* I'll send something Thursday, to reach you Saturday, and that will be all from me this week!"

To console them both, Carson offered an argument for the once-a-week letter: "During all these coming weeks when the miles separate us, there are, for both of us, ways in which we could turn them to constructive account. And to the extent that we do, I think we shall enrich and add to the joys of whatever periods of actual togetherness we can achieve this winter."

For eleven years, the women wrote to each other, eleven seasons of letter writing followed up by summers spent together on the island in Maine. At times, the weekly schedule was kept, with slight exceptions ("schedule or no schedule . . . a small note will go to you tomorrow"), while at other times, the schedule was completely discarded: "In this week when I thought I might go letterless until Friday, I've had three in four days! And such sweet ones."

Carson urged Freeman to write as often as she wished. "But please don't think of not-writing, when you think of something you want to tell me—for fear I'll think I have to rush to the typewriter and answer. I'll promise to think of the typewriter first."

Freeman responded, "I'm terribly torn—shall I pour out my soul as I usually do, or make this very short? If you'll promise you won't try to answer it, I'll probably go on at length. You see, I know what a temptation it is for me to want to answer at length, everything you say. And knowing you, I can believe you are tantalized in the same way, and I would spare you—or would I?"

The winters of writing back and forth and summers spent together by the sea ended when Rachel Carson died of cancer in April 1964, at the age of fifty-six. She had written one last letter, to be delivered posthumously. In that final letter, written over a series of days, Carson consoled her friend for what she knew would be coming grief: "What I want to write of is the joy and fun and gladness we have shared—for these are the things I want you to remember—I want to live on in your memories of happiness . . . Never forget, dear one, how deeply I have loved you all these years."

Freeman knew how deeply she had been loved, for she had loved back. And alongside their love and in between their letters, both women had lived full lives. Lives of huge impact and quiet impact, and lives with layers of family, responsibility, and escape. Lives of mundane duty ("Darling, I want to keep talking to you but I mustn't. I must try to pack books tonight"); of occasional primping ("I have only a few minutes, as I'm about to have a manicure"); and always taking time to notice the world around them: "The dawn chorus is in full swing here . . . At first it seemed only the robins—but a thousand of them saying 'Cheer up, Cheer up, Cheer up' with a rhythm . . . And [then] a wood thrush, so clear and bell-like. It was constant for a long while until finally an oriole threw in a few bubbles and the catbirds took up the main theme."

In between letters, life goes on. Birds sing, nails get done, illness is treated, and children grow up. Whereas life cannot be controlled—there is often more crying than singing, more dying than recovery, and more aging than growth—letters are within our charge. We can slow the pace, notice the details, and respond with thought and with heart.

It is not always easy waiting for a letter to arrive. But what joy when it does! As Mercy Otis Warren, the poet and historian of the American Revolution, wrote to her husband in September 1775, describing the letter she had just received from him: "No desert was ever more welcome to a luxurious palate, it was a regale to my longing mind: I had been eagerly looking for more than a week for a line from the best friend of my heart."

When I receive a letter, whether it is one I have been waiting for or an unexpected gift, I may not read it right away; I may want some quiet corner or moment to have the full enjoyment of reading it in full. I then place it in a special pile on my desk. I read it again, hours or days later. I think about what to write back. Days may pass, in which the letter replays itself in the back of my mind and my thoughts accumulate for refor-mulating, later, on paper. Because when someone writes to me, or when I write to someone, an instant response is not the expectation; instead, a thoughtful, rich reply is what we wait for. What we are willing to wait for.

I remember shoving an envelope into a mailbox once, almost snapping my wrist with the momentum. The vigorously mailed letter had been an angry response to a friend, answering her letter in which she accused me of not writing enough and of neglecting our friendship. We were both in college, separated by five states, and my angry letter back to her was fueled as much by guilt as by lack of sleep (this was college, after all).

Once I became calm, I grew repentant and I wanted my letter back again. I realized my friend was only asking me to make time for her, and as a friend, I should have. It was a sad comment on my friendship that I could find time to write in anger, and not in companionship. If only I had delayed my response, let time pass, before sending back my angry letter!

In July 1940, the writer Virginia Woolf received a letter from Ben Nicolson, son of her longtime friend and sometime lover Vita Sackville-West. Woolf had just published a biography about Roger Fry, an artist and member of the Bloomsbury Group. Young Nicolson was serving in the army, stationed in Kent and charged with launching anti-aircraft artillery at incoming German bombers. A budding art critic, he was fed up with what he saw as the Bloomsbury artists' failure to understand, much less address, the realities of war. In his scathing letter to Woolf, Nicolson claimed Fry had been out of touch after World War I, living in a "fool's paradise," and that "he shut himself out from all disagreeable actualities . . . [allowing] the spirits of Nazism to grow." Woolf wrote back a defense of Fry, asserting that he invited people to look at art and at life, and arguing: "Wasn't that the best way of checking Nazism?"

Nicolson wrote back, this time lashing out against the entire Bloomsbury group of artists and writers, of which Woolf was a member. Woolf quickly and angrily drafted a response, attacking Nicolson and questioning his usefulness as an art critic. But before she mailed her letter, she took a breath. She hesitated. Then she gave herself a day or two to think about Nicolson's argument. She rewrote her response to him, writing in a more conciliatory tone and offering thanks for their correspondence. A few months later, she wrote again to Nicolson, assuring him, "I love getting your letters . . . I'm so happy you found the life of Roger Fry interesting as well as infuriating." Her measured, well-spaced letters were enough to settle the waters between them. Neither party had changed their mind, but peace had been made.

Delay not only allows anger to cool, it also allows news to settle. When the lawyer and biographer James Boswell was courting the rich heiress

Catherine Blair, he had no time to write letters. But once she dumped him, he was able to write to his good friend the Reverend William Temple. The experience with Blair was now complete and could be described: "All is over between Miss Blair and me. I have delayed writing until I could give you some final account." Pages of the accounting follow, full of details about how the heiress treated both him and other suitors, and ending with the conclusion: "Now that all is over, I see many faults in her, which I did not see before."

Even then, Boswell delayed three days more before sending the letter off, after adding a postscript: "I have allowed my letter to lie till this day. The heiress is a good Scots lass. But I must have an English woman."

Edward Weeks was the longtime editor of the *Atlantic Monthly* (and, as editor, the first ever to publish a Hemingway short story, in 1927). He was outspoken on all sorts of issues, speaking out against television ("Why popularize stupidity?" he asked Mike Wallace during a 1958 interview), what he called "bigness" ("worship of bigness" is turning Americans into "mental pygmies"), and against censorship ("like the poor, it is always with us"). He was also a devoted letter writer.

In his 1955 collection of essays titled *The Open*

Heart, Weeks explained his devotion to the art of letter writing. Quoting E. V. Lucas, an early-twentieth-century collector of letters, who called letter writing "the gentlest art," Weeks went on to explain that such a gentle art offered the strongest of connections: letters "reflect the affectionate, high-spirited, often passionate individualism of men and women reaching across the silence of space for the sympathy of that other heart." Dorothy Freeman quoted that line in an October 1956 letter to Rachel Carson, writing it out in full and adding at the end "I love that last phrase." The sympathy of that other heart.

I like the whole sentence, but it is the phrase "the silence of space" that especially resonates. For me, the silence of space is the time that passes between letters sent and received. It is the place of living, of experience and emotion, a space for solitary thought. Yet the sympathy of the other heart is always there, in the letters I write and in the ones I wait for.

9

Correspondence Counseling

I always pass on good advice. It's the only
thing to do with it. It is never any use to
oneself.

—Oscar Wilde, *An Ideal Husband*

When I was twelve years old, I wrote to the
Barbizon School of Modeling. Enclosed
with the letter was a copy of my latest school
photo. The photo shows me smiling, blithely
unaware of both the disastrous state of my hair
and the remnants of lunch in my teeth (potato
chips and cheese sandwich, from the looks of it),
to say nothing of the impending bump upon my
nose.

I was not smiling when I wrote my letter to
Barbizon: "Please, can you help me?" I wrote in
desperation, "I am a disaster."

There is nothing new in asking strangers for
advice. Ancient Greeks from all walks of life
relied on the oracle at Delphi before doing
anything major, whether it was going to war or

traveling to Attica or pursuing love. Built over a crack in the ground that spewed hallucinogenic vapors, Apollo's temple at Delphi was like an ancient form of Skype between the Pythia (the priestess of the temple) and Apollo. The Pythia sucked up the fumes, received her visions from Apollo, and then shared what she had learned with the temple priests, wailing out her divinations from a special rock. It was then up to the priests to translate her ravings into beautifully constructed hexameters of advice, covering everything from government business to personal affairs to philosophical questions of life and death.

The most famous of the pronouncements received from the oracle is still well known today, and was inscribed at the time on the wall of the temple: *Know thyself.* But *how* do I get to know myself? And even more important, what should I do with my life, whom should I marry, where can I find satisfaction? And by the way, how can I avoid a bad hair day? Today we humans still have some serious questions we want answers to. In search of answers, we've gone from oracles to witches to sages to prophets, and then on to priests and confessors.

By the seventeenth century, the "agony aunts" were born, the distant ancestors of today's advice columnists. What a great idea, to dispense advice to the uncertain and the afflicted through the modem of the media. The first to seize on it was

John Dunton, a publisher and bookseller in London in the late 1600s, who set out to publish a newspaper devoted entirely to the giving of advice. Dunton solicited readers to send in queries to his *Athenian Mercury* about any confusing aspects of life, promising to resolve "all the most Nice and Curious questions proposed by the Ingenious."

Dunton's newspaper covered everything from grooming (although nothing about how to avoid a bad hair day) to courting (advising men to look for a woman "of soft, easie, affable Temper" and women to find an "Obedient husband") to sex (only within marriage).

Advice columns began popping up as features in newspapers throughout the eighteenth and nineteenth centuries, and still today, standards like "Dear Abby" and "Ask Ann Landers" play a vigorous role in offering advice to the public. Why do these columns do so well, utilizing the medium of anonymous letter and shared advice? Perhaps advice is more easily taken incognito, hiding the particulars of disgrace or shame or humility within the confines of a letter addressed to a stranger. Think about how often advice is sought for "a friend," when in fact, it is we who are looking for help with a tricky situation. The fake existence of a needy friend provides a state of forgiving anonymity.

The *giving* of advice, however, needs no

anonymity: most of us are quite eager to give advice openly and gratuitously, with full credit and glory due (to us). And what better mode for giving advice than through a letter? Whether our friends ask for advice or not, we give it freely and openly in our letters.

Wilkie Collins, one of my favorite writers (*The Woman in White* and *The Moonstone*), enjoyed a good life. Dickens was a best friend, two women loved him (he married neither but went back and forth between the two), and he had a busy career filled with writing, traveling, and expostulating. Despite the advantages of celebrity and success that he enjoyed, his health was altogether a different matter. Collins suffered for years from gout, trying out a number of remedies for relieving its worst symptoms. He eventually became addicted to laudanum. Despite (or perhaps because of) his bad health, Collins felt it was his duty to pen what he knew of good health, offering free advice to friends, as in the letter he wrote to Holman Hunt in 1848.

"The three rules of life that I find are the right ones," wrote Collins to Hunt, "are: 1. as much fresh air as possible . . . 2. live well—eat light *and* nourishing food, eggs, birds, fish, sweetbreads . . . find out the wine that agrees with you, and don't be afraid of it . . . 3. Empty your mind of your work before you go to bed—and don't let the work get in again until after breakfast the next morning . . ."

He added, "One last word . . . if you don't find that you make better progress . . . try my old friend, F. Carr Bear." In other words, *Try my advice, and if that doesn't work, try my doctor.*

Shirley Brooks, the editor of *Punch* magazine in nineteenth-century London, wrote a letter of advice to his old friend, the painter W. P. Frith, upon the occasion of Frith becoming a grandfather in the fall of 1865: "Begin to dress less jauntily, and wear a high waistcoat like the Right Reverend Bellew . . . avoid, so far, as thou canst, the taking [of] too much wine, [for] what thing is less dignified than a swipey Grandfather? . . . Buy a stick and practice walking with it, bending thy back, and not perking up elegantly when a comely female passeth by." And don't forget, Brooks added, "Leave off smoking, yet keep a box for thy younger friends who are not Grandfathers." Brooks wanted to be sure of a smoke when visiting his old friend.

Pliny the Younger, lawyer and writer in ancient Rome, wrote to a friend after visiting an old man by the name of Spurinna: "I am so much pleased with the uninterrupted regularity of his way of life, that if ever I should arrive at old age, there is no man whom I would sooner choose for my model."

Pliny then goes on with his newly gained wisdom on how to live a long life according to the Spurinna model: by following a regular schedule of long walks four times a day (and at least once a day in the nude, "if there happens to be no wind"), interspersed with reading and writing, riding out in a chariot, composing poetry, being read to while lounging on a couch, and enjoying "elegant yet frugal repast . . . served up in pure and antique plate."

Most wonderful of all, Pliny mentions that Spurinna plays daily "for a considerable time at tennis." This is advice I can most gladly follow. The "frugal" part of the meals I could also pull off, although I might not be able to serve it up elegantly and on the "pure and antique plate" used by Spurinna to such great advantage—and old age.

When Seneca, the ancient Roman philosopher, wrote to his friend Lucilius back in the first century, his advice on old age was less salubrious than Pliny's and more metaphysical: "Fruit is most grateful towards the end of the season . . . The past potation is the most agreeable to the lovers of wine; and every pleasure is most valued when it is coming to its end. Decay, when it is gradual, and not precipitate, is really pleasant . . . How sweet it is to have lived out, and taken leave of, all anxious desires!" His final sentence is one I will write into my journal of quotations, advice not just for a friend but for the ages: "He is the happiest man . . . who can go to bed at night saying, 'I have lived' . . . [and] rises every morning with a day gained."

Siblings are great ones for offering advice. Anne-Marie sent me cards when I was expecting my first child, reassuring me that I would be a good mother: "If you're as great a mother as you are a sister, Baby Menz is one lucky kid," she wrote, and advised me to have fun with it all. It was advice easy to follow (and assurance that a new mother needs).

In the early 1800s, Jeong Yak-yong of Korea wrote a long letter to his brother. Jeong Yak-yong is known today as Dasan, the great Confucian thinker, but around the end of the eighteenth century, Dasan and his older brothers had studied the precepts of Roman Catholicism, attracted by certain aspects of the religion. For their interests in Catholicism, they were persecuted by Queen Dowager Jeongsun, ruling monarch of Korea. Dasan and one brother were banished; their oldest brother was executed.

Living for years in exile on a desolate island, Dasan became an expert in surviving rough circumstances. In the winter of 1811, he sought to share that expertise with his brother Jeong Yak-jeon, living on another island not so far away. Concerned that Yak-jeon was not keeping his health up, Dasan admonished him against feeling squeamish about the local meat, arguing that the important thing is to eat whatever is necessary "to prolong your life"—even if the only meat available is dog: "On the island there are no less than a thousand or more wild dogs. If I were there, I would boil one every five days without fail."

Dasan goes on with practical details: "Take one ladleful of sesame, fry it up, and then crush into a powder. If there are onions in the garden and vinegar in the room, then we are ready for the dog." After all, "the Heavens made the isle of Huksan a fief of supplies for you and made meat available for eating. Wealth, distinction, and protection are provided, yet you choose to suffer. Isn't this being pedantic and inflexible?"

As Confucius said, "Faced with what is right, to leave it undone shows a lack of courage." Eat the dog, and stay alive.

Peter's brothers do not write to him at school, but I doubt they would offer recipes if they were to write, and certainly not anything to do with dogs. After all, the food at university is pretty good, and certainly ample. And as younger brothers, they might feel less qualified to offer advice to their older sibling, about food or studies or love. But if there were some topic they might want to offer their opinion on, to brother or to friend, my advice to them is: put it in a letter.

"Few take advice, or physic, without wry faces at it," wrote the brothers Augustus William Hare and Julius Charles Hare in their collection of aphorisms entitled *Guesses at Truth*, published in 1827. I agree wholeheartedly with the brothers that advice, no matter how easily given, is rarely easily taken. But by inserting a letter into the equation of giving counsel, the blow of implied criticism is softened, the threat of embarrassment is lessened (a letter does not blush), and the balm of concern is spread.

Katherine Mansfield, the great short story writer, married the editor John Middleton Murry in 1918. During their tumultuous years together, neither expected sexual fidelity from the other, and they openly enjoyed liaisons with other partners. But when Murry began an affair with the princess Elizabeth Bibesco in 1921, Bibesco broke what Mansfield considered a cardinal rule of polite behavior by writing love letters to her husband. (The princess must have learned the craft from her father, H. H. Asquith, the English prime minister who wrote all those love letters to Venetia Stanley.)

Mansfield could tolerate extramarital sex, but there was no way she could put up with the love letters. And so she wrote to the princess, offering some worthy advice: "I am afraid you must stop writing these little love letters to my husband while he and I live together. It is one of the things which is not done in our world . . . Please do not make me have to write to you again. I do not like scolding people and I simply hate having to teach them manners."

If Mansfield had taken on Princess Bibesco

face-to-face and demanded that she stop writing her love letters, an embarrassing scene for all parties might have ensued. By putting her advice in a letter, Mansfield saved face for herself and for the princess, and everyone stayed calm. Lesson taught and taken; there were no more love letters from Bibesco.

My letter to the Barbizon School of Modeling was answered. But the answer I got was not the one I expected. After all, Barbizon was not in the business of dispensing free advice. Instead, someone from the school contacted my mother and told her about my query. Perhaps the caller was trying to get my mother to sign up for costly modeling courses, but my mother wasn't buying.

I remember her calling me downstairs to tell me about the conversation with the woman from Barbizon. She gathered me in her arms and assured me that I was beautiful but, more importantly, that I was kind and smart and funny. She then brushed my hair, kissed my cheek, and sent me out to play. End of story, completion of intervention. I appreciated the words and the kiss, and I'm sure I had a great time outside, running around in the yard. But I could have used some lasting advice on personal presentation.

Philip Stanhope, 4th Earl of Chesterfield, would have been just the man to turn to for advice on personal grooming, and for anything else having to do with what he called "the graces" (and what Virginia Woolf called Chesterfield's "art of pleasing"). Always a man of style and grace (he had served as gentleman of the bedchamber to the Prince of Wales), Lord Chesterfield was quite certain about what matters most in life: to put on the best face possible, in all situations. Good grooming proves good breeding, and good breeding ensures all success.

Beginning around the year 1739, Chesterfield sent hundreds of letters to his illegitimate son Philip, hoping to guide the young man (the letters began when the boy was just seven years old) on the path of good education, best manners, and highest social standing. He advised his son freely on everything from the dangers of mindlessness— "It is a sure sign of a little mind to be doing one thing, and at the same time to be either thinking of another, or not thinking at all"—to the role of sexuality ("Making love becomes a General much better than a man of singular piety") to the value of competition: "When I was of your age, I should have been ashamed if any boy of that age had learned his book better, or played at any play better than I did; and I would not have rested a moment till I had got before him." (And all these bits of wisdom came when the poor boy was still under ten years old!)

As Stanhope grew, the letters of advice amplified and underscored and made clear the basic tenets of Chesterfield's code for living: to behave with "the air, the manners, the graces, and the style of the people of fashion." In concrete terms, that meant not only to exercise easy competence in "riding, fencing, and dancing" but to converse with confidence and good humor (albeit quietly: "A gentleman is often seen, but very seldom heard to laugh"). A man must be witty and interesting, but "never hold anybody by the button, or the hand, in order to be heard out; for if people are not willing to hear you, you had much better hold your tongue than them."

Flattery, advised Chesterfield, was usually a good course of action: "If a man has a mind to be thought wiser, and a woman handsomer, than they really are, their error is a comfortable one to themselves, and an innocent one with regard to other people; and I would rather make them my friends, by indulging them in it, than my enemies, by endeavoring . . . to undeceive them."

Guidance on sexual behavior became more explicit as Stanhope grew older ("An Iphigenia [an older woman] would both give you the desire, and teach you the means to please" and "Pleasing and governing women, may, in time be of great service to you . . . ."), but the message of behaving well and looking even better stayed simple: "Transcribe, imitate, emulate . . . exert your utmost care to acquire what people of fashion call shining."

Cynical, elegant, entertaining, and undeniably practical ("Talk often, but never long: in that case, if you do not please, at least you are sure not to tire your hearers"), Chesterfield's letters to his son had two goals: to teach Stanhope how to ensure his own popularity ("I want, that I and all the world should like you, as well as I love you"), and, perhaps more important, to assure the aging writer, whose own political and social powers had waned, that maintaining good face was all that mattered. Chesterfield admired a man who could age with grace and with dignity, much like his hero, the Duke of Marlborough: "He was always cool; and nobody ever observed the slightest variation in his countenance . . . With all his gentleness and gracefulness, no man living was more conscious of his situation, nor maintained his dignity better."

No food remnants in the teeth for Lord Chesterfield: "Many things must be suppressed, and many occasionally concealed in the best character . . . it is by no means necessary to show it all . . . leave it to your conduct, your virtues, your morals, and your manners [to demonstrate your best face]." I am certain he looked good, and behaved better, until the very end. And in the end, his only wish was a simple one: "All I desire, for my own burial, is not be buried alive."

Ben Franklin wrote often to his daughter Sally and took the opportunity to both scold her from afar—"Your sending for long black pins, and lace, and *feathers!* disgusted me as much as if you had put salt on my strawberries. The spinning I see, is laid aside and you are to be dressed for the ball! You seem not to know, my dear daughter, that of all the dear things in this world, idleness is the dearest, except mischief"—and to offer advice: "If you wear your cambric ruffles as I do and take care not to mend the holes, they will come in time to be lace; and feathers, my dear girl, may be had in America from every cock's tail."

When I think about the letters I have written to my children, I realize advice never has been big on my agenda. Perhaps I have not been worried enough, yet, to advise Peter in other than the most generic terms to work hard, eat well, and have fun; or perhaps I am not practiced enough (yet) in the art of writing advice to offspring in need of counsel. I have been rarely away from my kids, just a few trips here and there (during which I leave letters behind for them to open while I'm gone, assuring them of my love and reminding them to feed the cats) and no sleep-away camps in our past or in the foreseeable future.

It is in the separation between parent and child that worries surface, and it is often from worries that advice is born. Families writing to soldiers off at war send admonishments to eat enough, stay dry, keep your head down: "And when you do come marching home old fellow bring me back the same boy I gave my country—true, and clean, and gentle, and brave. You must do this for your father and me and Betty and Nora," wrote Kate Gordon, a mother of three boys sent to Europe during World War I. She added, with optimism, "And most of all, [do this] for the daughter you will give me one of these days! Dear, I don't know whether you have even met her yet—but never mind that!"

Lord Collingwood was an admiral in the Royal Navy during the Napoleonic Wars, away from home for years at a time. Known for his great seamanship and acuity in naval battles, as well as for his kindness and generosity (and for his opposition to then common practices of flogging and involuntary drafting into the army), Collingwood was called "father" by many of his sailors.

But his true children were the two girls he'd left at home, in the care of their mother: "I am sure I have great cause for thankfulness for such a family, a wife that is goodness itself, and two healthy children that with her care and her example can scarce fail to be like her. All my troubles here seem light when I look Northward and consider how well I am rewarded," he wrote to his friend Sir Edward Blackett in 1793.

Despite being so far away, Lord Collingwood wanted to play an integral role in the raising of his children and he wrote letters of counsel to his wife, offering ideas on how to educate the girls to stand strong against life's inevitable disappointments and disasters. He himself was suffering through the torments of war and of being away from wife and children for years—"If ever we have peace, I hope to spend my latter days amid my family, which is the only kind of happiness I can enjoy," and his advice is rooted in experience.

"How it would enlarge their mind, if they should acquire a sufficient knowledge of mathematics and astronomy to give them an idea of the beauty and wonders of creation!" he wrote to his wife on June 16, 1806 ("This day, my love, is the anniversary of our marriage and I wish you many happy returns of it"). He went on to write, "I would have my girls gain such knowledge of the works of the creation, that they may have a fixed idea of the nature of that Being who could be Author of such a world. Whenever they have that, nothing on this side of the moon will give them much uneasiness of mind . . . [for] they would then have a source of consolation for the worst that could happen."

Collingwood died at sea in 1810 and never made it home to England for his hoped-for "latter days" of happiness. The worst *had* happened, but with their father's advice the girls and their mother were able to endure it. They mined the wisdom found in his letters and looked to the wonders of the world for consolation.

Bud Wilkinson, the legendary coach of the Oklahoma Sooners football team, sent off weekly letters to his son Jay in the early 1960s. Jay was a student at Duke, playing football for the Blue Devils and struggling to keep up with the university's academic rigors. In Jay's first year of college, his father wrote to him imparting not only fatherly wisdom but adding in a bit of multi-generational advice as well: "My grandmother, a great lady—one of the finest I've ever known—always told me when I was a young boy growing up 'dare to be a Daniel; dare to stand alone.' . . . Only in this way can you find peace of mind because you cannot be happy doing 'what other people think you should do.'"

As a winning football coach and father to a devoted player, it was natural that many of Wilkinson's letters were about football. I was surprised that his emphasis wasn't on winning but on the "fundamentally educational" aspect of playing football—"It isn't winning or losing that has lasting value or importance . . . the loyalty, the joys, the disappointments, and above all learning to give your TOTAL best mentally, emotionally, and physically. These are the qualities that will make a man."

In the end, what Wilkinson wanted was what all parents want, for his son to be happy: "My advice, for what it's worth, is to live fully and well . . .

without worry, concern or guilt feelings of any kind . . . Have balance in your life of study, expression, prayer, service, fun, recreation, and frivolity . . . the future belongs to you. It will be brighter than the stars."

Like all parents, I hope that my children can find balance in their lives, calm over discord, happiness over strife, and endurance over despair. As the poet W. B. Yeats wrote in "A Prayer for My Daughter," he hoped his baby daughter Anne would grow up to someday understand that she could, "though every face should scowl / And every windy quarter howl / Or every bellows burst, be happy still."

Yeats offered advice through poems, while his letters to the growing Anne tended to be mundane stuff, such as: "See the croquet ground is in order. I shall I think be home in about ten days." And praising her always on her letter writing: "You write a good, lively letter. Thank you." A wise father, to encourage by positive reenforcement the habit of letter writing.

Perhaps I *should* be offering advice to Peter through my letters. I have, after all, been in college, drunk a few beers, fallen in and out of love, studied hard and played much and traveled far, married a good man and raised good kids. I have experience and knowledge worth imparting.

F. Scott Fitzgerald wrote often to his daughter Scottie, away at camp or school. Financial problems sent him to Hollywood to eke out a living (this was long before *The Great Gatsby* became an international favorite). Scottie stayed on the East Coast, first in boarding school and then in college at Vassar. Fitzgerald always emphasized that his letters of advice were to be read not once, but twice, to ensure her understanding: "*Please,* turn back and read this letter over! It is too packed with considerable thought to digest the first time."

Despite Fitzgerald's repeated pleas to read carefully and then to read again ("Will you please read this letter a second time? I wrote it over twice"), Scottie admits that at the time she was mainly looking for enclosed checks and gossipy news in the letters her father sent. But she did save each and every letter, in her lower-right-hand desk drawer: "I knew they were great letters . . . I saved them the way you save *War and Peace* to read."

Fitzgerald's most famous letter to Scottie is the one in which he lists things to worry about (courage, cleanliness, efficiency, horsemanship) and things not to worry about (the past, the future, flies, mosquitoes, insects in general, parents, boys, disappointments), and concluding with a list of things to think about: "What am I really aiming at?"; "Do I really understand people?"; and "Am I trying to make my body a useful instrument or am I neglecting it?"

But the advice I like best in Fitzgerald's letters

has been polished through his own experience: "It's all right to like affection, but not when you drive . . . I simply don't want you in danger and I don't want you to do anything inappropriate for your age. For premature adventure one pays an atrocious price . . . every boy I know who drank at eighteen or nineteen is now safe in his grave. The girls who were what we called 'speeds' at sixteen were reduced to anything they could get at marrying time."

Harsh advice, but Fitzgerald the dad is doing all he can to keep his daughter, on the other side of the continent from him, in line. Having written novels about flappers, he knows he does not want one for a daughter: "I don't want you to live in an unreal world . . . Every girl your age in America will have the experience of working for her living . . . to say 'I will do valuable and indispensable work' is the part of wisdom and courage."

Fitzgerald was often practical: "If for one week you put each thing away individually from the moment of touching it to the moment of its final disposal—instead of putting away three things at a time—I think that you would lick it [messiness] in a month and life would be easier for you." Pick up your clothes off the floor, girl, and get on with it.

And he was witty: "This job [script writing in Hollywood] has given me part of the money for your tuition. . . . I hate to see you spend it on a course like 'English Prose Since 1800.' Anybody that can't read modern English prose by themselves is subnormal—and you know it."

But most of all, Fitzgerald's letters to his daughter are honest about his outlook on life, both in general—"Life is essentially a cheat and its conditions those of defeat, and that the redeeming things are not 'happiness and pleasure' but the deeper satisfactions that come out of struggle"— and in particular: "You have got two beautiful bad examples for parents. Just do everything we didn't do and you will be perfectly safe."

Marie de l'Incarnation left her twelve-year-old son (her husband had died just after the boy's birth) to journey from Tours, France, to the New World in 1639. She traveled to the great wilderness driven by her dreams of God and converts, and with the goal of establishing an Ursuline convent and school in the village of Quebec. Burdened by harsh weather conditions, devastating illnesses ("smallpox . . . spread to our seminary, which in a very few days resembled a hospital . . ."), a fire in 1650 that destroyed almost everything (she would write later of finally understanding, while standing in the midst of the fire, the "nothingness" of things), and periodic lack of food and supplies (relying on eels for their only sustenance at times), Marie persevered. She learned at least three Native languages, taught hundreds of French and Native girls to read and write, and documented the growth of Quebec into a bustling town in the letters she wrote to benefactors back in France.

She also wrote hundreds of letters to her son Claude, advising him on his own religious path and cheering him forward toward what she was sure was sainthood, if not martyrdom ("See to what extent I love you that I wish you should be worthy to spill your blood for Jesus Christ"). But the most moving letter in all the years of writing to Claude was the one she wrote in response to his expression of doubt and anguish. "We see nothing, we walk gropingly, and . . . ordinary things do not come about as they have been foreseen and advised," she sympathized. She then counseled her son, "Just when one thinks oneself at the bottom of an abyss, one finds oneself on one's feet."

The promise of resilience, offered by parent to child: just when all seems lost, we find our way. Marie offered her advice to Claude across thousands of miles, through a simple and loving letter. The school established by Marie still operates today in Quebec City, standing on the same spot where Marie built the first walls. And her letters of advice to Claude survive as well, underscored by her last words before she died: "Tell him I carry him with me in my heart."

Madame de Sévigné and her daughter, Marie-

Françoise, wrote back and forth to each other all their lives, separated at times by a few miles and at other times by an entire country. Madame de Sévigné was a financially independent woman of society and her daughter was married to a French nobleman with money troubles and a flair for luxury living. Mother and daughter floundered and flourished within the ambit of the court of Louis XIV, and wrote about their adventures (and misadventures) in great detail.

Madame de Sévigné wrote not only to record the gossip, news, and forecasts of her social circle, but also to dispense advice to her grown child, on everything from health ("This is the third year in a row you have been in labor in November. It will be September, next year, if you do not control him [the husband] . . . you have suffered more than if you had been broken on the wheel") to finances ("What folly, my bonne, to have four people in your kitchen! Why so many, and what's to become of you with such expenses . . . And on top of that, to have three valets! In your household, it is always double or triple anyone else's!"); and from how to care for babies ("Those boils you describe . . . seem to me a bad sign") to how to provide for a child's future (advising against the convent, as it was too much like a "prison").

Of all the advice Madame de Sévigné offered her daughter my favorite is on the subject of motherhood: "Love, love your daughter, my dear child; it is the most natural and delightful occupation in the world."

Yes, loving my children has been the most natural and delightful occupation of my life. And it is natural, as well, to want to write letters of advice to those children whom we love so much. I have been good at writing letters of love to my children—the notes I leave when I go away for a day, the birthday cards and the Post-its I put in lunch bags, and the letters I write to Peter off at school—but it might be time to offer written advice now. What advice would I give?

Live in wonder. Remember joy. Stand still long enough to notice beauty. The ability to listen is just as important as the facility to speak. Read a lot, from all the different stacks in the library. Don't listen to very loud music on your headphones. Eat breakfast (an ongoing debate in our family is over which is the most important meal of the day—hands down, in my opinion, it is breakfast). Change the sheets on your bed every week. Meet your professors, ask questions you don't know the answers to, sign up for something new every once in a while—but stay away from the illegal, the illicit, the ill-conceived, and anyone with a bad cold.

And *how* to write my letters of advice? Simple. Pen to paper, stamp to envelope, and hope on the wing: that the letter arrives, and the chosen child reads it.

Lord Chesterfield acknowledged that parents' letters often go ignored, as "the advice of parents . . . is ascribed to the moroseness, the imperiousness, or the garrulity of old age." I hope Peter doesn't find me morose or imperious; rather, I worry he thinks that I just don't have a clue. But I should jump in anyway and share what advice I have. A letter allows me to offer it all, without interruption and without viewing the annoyance or boredom of the one to whom the advice is offered.

In fact, Peter may just take my advice more easily for not having to face me, but in being allowed to take in the advice on his own terms, in private, and in controllable slots of time. He can read and disregard, as he wishes. But he can also read my letters, save them, and return to my words of wisdom, as needed. Stick them in a desk drawer, my son, but don't forget they are there: letters of advice, underscored by love.

10

Leaving Words Behind

> A letter always feels to me like immortality because it is the Mind alone without corporeal friend.
>
> *—Emily Dickinson,*
> *letter to T. W. Higginson*

Years ago, I received a postcard from a friend traveling from New York City to his hometown of San Francisco. Doug was my close confidant in matters of the heart, my utter superior in Scrabble, and my coconspirator in naps taken under the desk in the office we shared: one of us stayed awake guarding the door while the other snoozed. When Doug first started having stomach problems, we never imagined it would be cancer. Now he was driving cross-country, cruising along home to San Francisco in a shiny red convertible.

Doug's postcard came from the road, a jam-packed scribbled note about the glories of small-town USA, some of the people he'd met and strange sights he'd seen, and details about a little car trouble he'd had in the Mid-Atlantic states. In the entire hundred-plus-word missive that Doug managed to fit on the three-by-five card, there was not the slightest nod to the cancer consuming his body. He and I had had that conversation, a few times, and Doug wanted our final communications to be about life. His postcard to me was a salvo shot in the battle for joy against all odds, and Douglas Blakeman was firing on all cylinders.

Doug is still in my life in so many ways, my memories and my photos. But his letters are the physical connection between us. Our shared past comes alive in letters: moments brought to life, re-created, replayed.

Most of the letters that I read today were written by people who have died. I still get some letters in the mail, but the collections that I cull from, gathered in books or archives or a friend's attic, make up the bulk of my reading. Through these letters I meet people, many of them not very famous people, who lived before me, buzzing along with their particular worries or fears or dreams. Through their letters, these writers come into their own, both in their time and mine.

The word "stationery" comes from the name of the shopkeepers who first sold it, centuries ago: stationery (writing paper) sold by the stationer, a medieval term used for a tradesman who had a standing (stationary) shop versus a vendor who traveled around with wares to sell. Presence is inferred in the word "stationery" and permanence is as well. When my physical self is gone, my physical letters can survive. I am here for you, says a letter, and I always will be.

I think back to the marvelous Addie Brown, who loved her Rebecca so fully and so beautifully through her letters of the mid-1800s, or to Heloise in her convent. Would I know these women and their lives any other way than through their letters? If Rebecca Primus had not saved Addie's letters, I would not have made her acquaintance; if Heloise had not written her letters, I might only know of her through Abelard's distorted view, as presented in his letter of consolation to a friend. But through their letters, the women are stationed forever in time. To be found by me, in my time.

"My Old Master," wrote Jourdan Anderson in 1865, "I have often felt uneasy about you. I thought the Yankees would have hung you long before this, for harboring Rebs they found at your house. I suppose they never heard about your going to Colonel Martin's to kill the Union soldier that was left by his company in their stable." Jourdan wrote his letter in response to his former owner's request that he return to the old farm in Tennessee now that the Civil War had ended and resume working for his old master.

But Jourdan has not forgotten that "you shot at me twice before I left you" or that "Henry intended to shoot me if he ever got a chance." As for coming "home again," Jourdan is clear: "Now if you will write and say what wages you will give me, I will be better able to decide whether it would be to my advantage to move back again." His wife, Mandy—"they call her Mrs. Anderson here"—is fearful of Anderson's intentions and so "we have concluded to test your sincerity by asking you to send us our wages for the time we served you. This will make us forget and forgive old scores, and rely on your justice and friendship in the future. I served you faithfully for thirty-two years, and Mandy twenty years . . . deduct what you paid for our clothing, and three doctor's visits to me, and pulling a tooth for Mandy, and the balance will show what we are in justice entitled to . . . If you fail to pay us for faithful labors in the past, we can have little faith in your promises in the future."

Jourdan admonishes his old Master—"We trust the good Maker has opened your eyes to the wrongs which you and your fathers have done to me and my fathers, in making us toil for you for generations without recompense"—and vows to protect his family against any such evils done under the name of slavery: "Please state if there would be any safety for my Milly and Jane, who are now grown up, and both good-looking girls. You know how it was with poor Matilda and Catherine. I would rather stay here and starve—

and die, if it come to that—than have my girls brought to shame by the violence and wickedness of their young masters. You will also please state if there has been any schools opened for the colored children in your neighborhood. The great desire of my life now is to give my children an education, and have them form virtuous habits."

Jourdan Anderson ends his letter with a jab of humor—"Say howdy to George Carter, and thank him for taking the pistol from you when you were shooting at me"—but never backs down: Jourdan owns his life now, and no one can take that dominion away, ever. Through his letter, his freedom is forever affirmed.

Anthony Chase, writing well before the Civil War, wrote to explain why he ran away from his owner: "What can a man do who has his hands bound and his feet fettered . . . He will certainly try to get them loosened by fair and Honorable means and if not so he will certainly get them loosened in any way that he may think most adviseable." Chase promised to send payment for the lost "property" (himself): "As soon as I can accumulate a sum of money suficent I will remit it . . . to prove to the world that I dont mean to be dishonest but wish to pay her every cent that I think my services is worth."

A Baltimore widow owned Chase and had refused to allow him to buy his freedom, despite Chase's assertion that he had been promised such freedom upon the death of his owner. Instead, the widow reneged on her husband's promise and hired Chase out to another man, Jeremiah Hoffman. In his letter, written to Hoffman, Chase is more concerned about his own honesty (willing to pay his purchase price) than with questioning the right of slave ownership in the first place. At the time he wrote in 1827, emancipation was more than a quarter century down the road, and under the law, Chase had stolen property.

He wrote to Hoffman, "I dont suppose that I shall ever be forgiven for this act but I hope to find forgiveness in the world that is to com." Little did he know that he would find much more than forgiveness in the days to come, when people like me read his letter and wonder at his bravery and his certainty: "I dont take this step mearly because I wish to be free but because I want to do justice to myself and to others."

In 1858, Abream Scriven was sold by his owner, the Reverend Charles Colcock Jones, to a trader by the name of Peterson. Peterson's plans were to take Scriven to New Orleans and sell him away again, moving him yet farther and farther away from his wife and children still living on Jones's plantation in rural Georgia. Scriven wrote to his wife of the trader's plans and then penned his farewells: "Give my love to my father & mother and tell them good Bye for me. and if we Shall not meet in this world I hope to meet in heaven. My

Dear wif for you and my Children my pen cannot express the griffe [grief] I feel to be parted from you all I remain your truly husband until Death."

For this one letter that survives, how many thousands of others suffered the same anguish of parting, against their will, from those they loved most on earth? How apt Scriven's name, ensuring that none who read his letter would ever forget. In 1795, a slave by the name of Judith Cocks wrote to James Hillhouse, a United States senator from Connecticut. Hillhouse was an early leader in the antislavery movement, declaring to Congress: "I consider slavery as a serious evil and wish to check it wherever I have authority." Cocks was an indentured slave, a situation for African slaves that was more common in the 1700s; her slavery had a supposed time limit, and she harbored hopes of becoming free and of releasing her children from slavery as well. At the time of the letter, Cocks needed Hillhouse's help to release "my little son Jupiter . . . my greatest care" from indentured servitude to Mrs. Woodbridge, a woman who "allows all her sons to thump and beat him the same as if he were a dog."

Cocks's letter lists all the ways she has worked hard, and how it has been necessary to battle unjust accusations lodged against her by Mrs. Woodbridge: "She has calle me a thief and I denie . . . I have don my duty as I could do here and all her family as well as my strength wold allow . . . I have not ronged her nor her family." She closes her plea for assistance with the statement "This is my handwriting." Her writing, her testimony, to be preserved for centuries. The cares of a mother, caught in an unjust system of servitude and powerlessness. But in some wonderful way, power is returned to her through words made with her own hand.

In November 1840, Joseph Taper wrote a letter to be forwarded on from a friend to his old master. Taper was writing from his new home in Saint Catharines, Canada, not far from Niagara Falls. Life had been good for him in Canada: "Since I have been in the Queen's dominions, I have been well contented. Yes well contented for sure, man is as God intended he should be. That is, all born free & equal. This is a wholesome law, not like the Southern laws which puts man made in the image of God, on level with the brutes . . . Would that the 5th verse of the 3d chapter of Malachi were written with the pen of iron & the point of a diamond upon every oppressors heart that they might repent of this evil, & let the oppressed go free."

He writes that he only left the United States because of "bad usage: only for that, & I should have been in America, though I do not regret coming, & if I had known how easy I could get along I should [have] started 10 years sooner, for it would have been better for me. Besides having a good garden, this summer I raised 316 bushels of potatoe, 120 bushels corn, 41 bushels buckwheat, a small crop of oats, 17 hogs, 70 chickens."

At the end of his letter, Taper writes, "My wife and self are sitting by a good comfortable fire happy, knowing that there are none to molest or make afraid. God save Queen Victoria. The Lord bless her in this life, & crown her with glory in the world to come."

A lovely picture, Taper warm by the fire with his wife, the crops set away for winter, hogs and chickens content in their sheds.

The only document that remains to testify to the life of the slave Vilet Lester is a letter she wrote in 1857 to her former mistress in North Carolina. Vilet recounts all the owners she has had through the years—"whend I left Randolf I went to Rockingham and Stad there five weaks and then I left there and went to Richmon virgina to be Sold and I Stade there three days and was bought by a man by the name of Groover and braught to Georgia and he kept me about Nine months and he being a trader Sold me to a man by the name of Rimes and he Sold me to a man by the name of Lester and he has owned me four years and Says that he will keep me til death Siperates us without Some of my old north Caroliner friends wants to buy me again."

Vilet is anxious for news of the family she left unwillingly behind: "Never befour did I [k]no[w] what it was to want to See a parent and could not. I wish you to gave . . . my manafold love to mother brothers and sister and pleas to tell them to Right to me So I may here from them if I cannot See them."

Most of all, Vilet wants to know, "What has Ever become of my Presus little girl. I left her in goldsborough with Mr. Walker and I have not herd from her Since and Walker Said that he was going to Carry her to Rockingham and gave her to his Sister and I want to [k]no[w] whether he did or no as I do wish to See her very mutch." Vilet's current owner is willing to buy Vilet's daughter but "he wishes a answer as Soon as he can get one as I wis him to buy her an my Boss being a man of Reason and fealing wishes to grant my trubled breast that mutch gratification and wishes to [k]now whether he will Sell her now."

There is no existing document to show that Vilet ever was reunited with her daughter or any other members of her family. But her letter endures, rendering both mother and daughter neither anonymous nor forgotten.

An American soldier named Arian Edwards wrote to his mother during World War II. Stationed in France, and "about to go into battle," Edwards wrote in anticipation of the worst outcome: "I . . . have instructed the company clerk to send you this letter in case I become a casualty

. . . receipt of this letter by you will indicate I am either with God or a prisoner in the hands of the enemy." The message he wants to convey to his mother is clear: "War was absolutely necessary on the part of my country, and although I was thirty-four years old and nobody expected me to go, yet some one had to go; someone must make the sacrifice, some mother must lose her son."

Edwards seeks to reassure his mother: "I . . . have never for one moment regretted my decision, and I will not . . . Life is not the highest boon of existence. There are ideals that are superhuman, interests greater than life itself, for which it is worth fighting, suffering and dying."

He ends his letter with "Good-bye Mother; I will see you in the next world. You may know I died fighting for you, my country, and all that life holds dear."

He died just days after writing to his mother and his letter was sent home. Was his mother reassured by his words? She might have found some comfort in knowing that his letter, saved and shared, would endow him with a kind of immortality.

During the Anglo-Zulu War in the late 1800s, the parents of a young English soldier sent off across the world to fight received a letter from their son. Private Ashley Goatham counseled his parents, "Never mind about me. I hope to pull through all safe by the help of God . . . So, my dear mother, cheer up. Time might come when I shall come home and surprise the lot."

Goatham never made it home to the small village of Bredgar in Kent; he was killed at Isandlwana, Africa, on January 29, 1879, at the age of twenty-four. But the image of a smiling Ashley, coming in through the back door, ready to give his mum a hug, endures, through his letter.

Jack Trice was the first black student to play football for Iowa State College. During his first major football game, against the University of Minnesota in Minneapolis in October 1923, Trice suffered a broken collarbone in the first quarter. Despite the pain, Trice refused to sit it out. He played on through to the third quarter, when he was thrown on his back and trampled by three Minnesota players. Trice was taken off the field and sent to the hospital, where doctors declared him fit to travel back to Iowa. Two days later Trice died from hemorrhaged lungs and internal bleeding as a result of the injuries he received during the game with Minnesota. He left behind family, a fiancée, and the more than four thousand fellow students and faculty who attended his funeral, shaken by shock and grief.

Just before Trice was buried, a letter was found in the pocket of his suit jacket. It was a letter he had written to himself the night before the Minnesota game: "My thoughts just before the first real college game of my life: The honor of my race, family & self is at stake. Everyone is expecting me to do big things. I will. My whole body and soul are to be thrown recklessly about the field tomorrow . . . Fight low, with your eyes open and toward the play . . . Be on your toes every minute if you expect to make good. Jack."

The football stadium of Iowa State University is now called the Jack Trice Stadium. In front of the stadium there is a bronze statue of Trice, standing with one knee up, foot resting on a ledge, head bent down, reading a letter he holds in his hand. The letter he wrote to himself, his last.

James Russell Lowell was famous for his poetry, and for his work as an abolitionist in the years leading up to the Civil War. Martin Luther King Jr. often quoted from Lowell's poem "The Present Crisis"; his favorite lines were "Truth forever on the scaffold, Wrong forever on the throne, / Yet that scaffold sways the future, and, behind the dim unknown / Standeth God within the shadow, keeping watch above his own."

Lowell's last letters, written in the months before his death in 1891, offer an enduring presence different from that he got through his poetry: "It is raining faintly to-day, with a soft southerly wind which will prevail with the few leaves left on my trees to let go their hold and join their fellows on the ground. I have forbidden them to be raked away, fore the rustle of them stirs my earliest memories, and when the wind blows they pirouette so gaily as to give me cheerful thoughts of death."

He writes about the changes around him: "I hardly know the old road (a street now) that I have paced for so many years . . . [and yet] The two old English elms in front of the house haven't changed . . . a trifle thicker in the waist, perhaps, as is the wont of prosperous elders, but looking just as I first saw them seventy years ago, and it is a balm to my eyes." And he comments on the passage of life, his and all of ours: "How artificial a contrivance Time is. We have Eternity given us in the lump, can't believe in such luck, and cut it up into mouthfuls as if it wouldn't go round so many. Are we to be seduced by the superstitious observances of the earth and sun into a belief in days and years?"

Lowell is right. We can hold on to certain moments forever through the writing of a letter. English elms, standing against the wind: the experience is still vibrant to us—alive!—through reading Lowell's letters.

The enduring experience can be dramatic, as when the Brazilian writer Joaquim Maria Machado de Assis wrote his last letter to an old friend ("My dear friend, I read a few pages . . . of Flaubert. I found the same solitude and sadness that I have, and even the same sickness . . . Farewell . . . an embrace from your old friend")—a rare admission of his epilepsy and a lasting testament to their friendship—or it can be simple, as when M. F. K. Fisher wrote a casual note to a friend in 1979, describing a meal she'd made for Japanese visitors:

"I had some good beef stock, and plenty of herbs and scallions and mushrooms and some Italian tomatoes, and I produced a really nice thing . . . a bed of coarsely chopped watercress and a lot of a very stiff aspic loaded with paperthin vegetables . . . We ate a huge platter of it, with two kinds of bread, and then strawberries and cookies."

In another letter, Fisher describes a meal she had by herself, out on an "attic balcony" in Paris in the 1960s: "I ate a big tureen of fresh soup and a pile of good strawberries and drank a bottle of wine on my own." My stomach grumbles and mouth waters. Moments don't have to be heroic to be memorable; even the plainest of details renders the time present and enduring.

Sarah McClendon was a pioneer in the late 1700s, leaving her native North Carolina to settle in the wilds of northwest Kentucky. Her surviving letters, passed down through generations of McClendons, create a vivid picture of life on the frontier. In 1797 she wrote to her family back home in North Carolina, telling them to "kuit worreng bout us not havin plenty to eat. We hade boiled wild geese, wild plum puddin, wild cherry perserves, corn bred, cracked hominy, wild greens, roaster deer, dandelions, beaten white bred, goseberry purserves made with honey, hog meat, milk, butter, kottage cheze, gravy, mushrons."

The labors required to get all the food together are implied in her letters but never belabored, as she assures her family, "I never want for help. Benjamin is good to me, he still calls me Love, and I have a surprise now do not worry bout me. I am in the family way with my first baby, Benjamin say it makes him love me more, but I do not see how he could love me more . . . I never was in better health in all my life."

Babies would come and families would flourish in McClendon's corner of Kentucky: "I know you hated for us to leave but we never wish we had not . . . God helps us, sometime he send the deer and buffalo by so we can have meet when the snow is awful deep, he send the snow bird to chirp to us with the hail covered trees swaying crackling poping with music, the bright sun coming up through the tree tops no place but heaven could be prettyr than this, the eagle and birds flying or setting in the tree tops with there music wabbles."

Sarah wrote in a letter, years later, "I just keep whistling Yankee Doodle Dandy." Yankee Doodle, keep it up: and Sarah McClendon did, preserving her pioneer life through her letters.

In the green trunk where I save my postcards and letters, there is an old Godiva chocolate box decorated with pink and green flowers and fastened with a pink ribbon. In this box I keep the scraps of notes my children have written me over the years. One of the oldest is from Peter, written during his third summer: a torn piece of yellow legal paper, covered with pen scribbles. Written below the scribbles, in my own handwriting, are the words "Peter says this is a letter to me, saying that he loves me 'so much.'" I read the note and tears come: the love is still there, although the boy has grown up.

More tears—a different emotion—when I pull Doug's postcard from the trunk. I imagine the two of us, side by side in his red convertible. The top is down, wind whipping my hair around until I tie it back. The cornfields of Indiana go by in a green blur as we listen to the Rolling Stones and "(I Can't Get No) Satisfaction," again and again. We sing along together, louder and louder. Doug, through his card, is forever my friend beside me.

11

To End with Love

A la tarde de la vida, te examinarán en el
amor.
(At the end of life, we shall be judged by
love.)

—San Juan de la Cruz

Sullivan Ballou of the Union army wrote to his wife during the early months of the Civil War, promising her that "my love for you is deathless, it seems to bind me with mighty cables that nothing but omnipotence can break . . . If I do not return, my dear Sarah, never forget how much I loved you." He then offered his hope that "the dead can come back to this earth and flit unseen around those they love, [for then] I shall always be with you, in the brightest day and in the darkest night . . . always, always. And when the soft breeze fans your cheek, it shall be my breath, or the cool air your throbbing temple, it shall be my spirit passing by."

One week later Ballou died in the first Battle of Bull Run. But his promise had been made, and letter sent.

Mike Royko and Carol Duckman grew up together, living close by each other on Chicago's North Side. By age ten Mike was in love with Carol, but Carol had other fish to fry. When Mike enlisted in the air force in 1952, Carol became engaged to another man. Mike went to Korea and Carol got married.

Then one day Mike got a letter from Carol. She told him she had separated from her husband; the marriage had been "a mistake." Mike wrote back in double time, admitting his long-held feelings for her: "I'm in love with you . . . For a couple of years I wondered when I would stop thinking about you every day. I've come to the conclusion that I won't. So as long as I have to keep going this way you may as well know about it."

It took the courage of a letter—hers, then his—to finally unveil his feelings: "I've been in love with you for so long, I don't remember when it started but when I decided to do something about it, it was too late."

Carol wrote back—it was not so late after all—and the two began exchanging letters, passionate ones on his behalf, and tentative ones on hers. But Mike didn't mind: "I haven't kidded myself into thinking that you might feel the same way I do. This isn't the first time that a love has been one sided."

Carol's affections grew, and Mike's joy blossomed: "Your letters have not only made me the happiest guy alive, but they have actually improved my golf game. This afternoon I came down from cloud nine long enough to shoot the best game I've ever had . . . Right now I feel that nothing is impossible, nothing unattainable."

"Absence lessens half hearted passions and increases great ones, as the wind puts out the candles and yet stirs up the fire," he promised Carol. Still in the air force but now stationed in Blaine, Washington, Mike was closer than before but halfway across the country. But distance could not matter: "They say that a sincere love increases with time, so until tomorrow when I'll love you more than I do today."

After six months of corresponding, he was given a few days off to come home. Mike and Carol were reunited. They had three days and by the end of leave, they were engaged.

"I won't be the smartest, richest, or best-looking husband in the world, but there won't be anyone who loves his wife more than I love you," Mike wrote to Carol when he got back to Blaine. "Baby, some people are born under lucky stars. My star was cloudy for a while but it's shining brightly now. That night, that wonderful, memorable, historic night you said you loved me was the turning point of my life . . . My whole life is in your hands, your beautiful hands. I love you, my darling, my sweetheart, my wife."

Another leave of a few days in November, and

the couple were married. They met in Olympia, Washington, for the ceremony and spent the honeymoon, measured in hours, in a hotel close by.

With Carol back in Chicago once again, and Mike back in Blaine, he wrote to his new wife, "I'm miserable because we're apart, yet I feel great whenever I look at my ring and realize we are married. Most of my time has been spent in reliving our honeymoon and thinking of how wonderful you are."

Finally, in January 1955 Mike was transferred to the air force base at O'Hare Airport, to a job that would lead him to writing for the Chicago papers and eventually becoming a nationally syndicated columnist. It was the beginning: Mike was coming home to his Carol, to his city, to his career as a writer. He wrote, "Just a few more days and we'll be together. 'Til then, I love you always."

Twenty-two years later, in September 1977, on Mike's birthday, Carol died of a brain aneurysm. For the first time in two decades of being a daily columnist, Royko couldn't write a thing. Weeks passed. And then he published a short story for his column. Titled "A November Farewell," the story was about a man and a woman who spend their weekends at a cottage on "a small, quiet Wisconsin lake." From the deck of their cottage, together they watch countless sunsets: "Whatever they were doing, they'd always stop to sit on the pier or deck and silently watch the sun go down, changing the color of the lake from blue to purple to silver and black."

But then the woman dies. The man has to pack up the house and he does so one November day, as fast as he can. But "he didn't work quickly enough. He was still there at sunset . . . He tried but he couldn't watch it alone. Not through tears. So he turned his back on it, went inside, drew the draperies, locked the door, and drove away without looking back."

Royko had packed up the lake cottage and put away the love letters. For years, all Royko's two boys knew about their parents' love story was what they'd glimpsed in "November Farewell." Their mother had told them about the letters written back and forth during the war, but never offered any details. Then, after Royko died in 1997, his son David found a box in his father's closet, containing the letters the couple had exchanged.

For David it was like "the holy grail of my nuclear family. The place where it all began." David found the place where it all still existed: the love and the young lovers on the pages of their letters.

Georgia O'Keeffe and Alfred Stieglitz exchanged over twenty-five thousand pages of letters during their thirty-one-year relationship. For years those letters were kept locked away, under the terms of O'Keeffe's will. Finally, in 2011, the first volume of selected letters was published. When I read them—over seven hundred pages—I was enchanted, pacing myself through the pages of letter after letter: "First I thought I wanted you to kiss me—hold me in your arms a moment before I go out into the sunshine—then—that didn't seem enough—I wanted you to touch all of me—everywhere," O'Keeffe wrote to Stieglitz early in their attachment.

Stieglitz wrote to O'Keeffe, "Your letter is a marvel & it has worked me all up . . . for my life was never more intense—terrifically concentrated and . . . Fearless . . . another wonderful living bit of flesh & blood of yours in the shape of a letter."

"I had four letters from you yesterday—It was a great treat—They were very sweet and dear," wrote O'Keeffe. "I keep them right by my side on my table so I can touch them and read them when I want to."

The letters underscored their separations ("Please don't—for awhile—write me those letters that always knock me down—Sometimes your letters are so much yourself—such an intense live sort of self that I can't stand yourself—and myself too," wrote O'Keeffe) but were also the means of staying close across the miles, as when Stieglitz wrote to O'Keeffe, "Your letter of this morning is another real joy—Full of sea breezes" and "I wonder when you'll get this scribble—I hope some time before evening . . . It brings you millions—billions of kisses—quiet and passionate ones—an assortment unheard of—"

I feel the ardor in the letters: "It is not your body," Stieglitz wrote, "nor even lips—or hands—which make you what you are for me—there is an equality between us. I need you—as you need me . . . the contact of souls—or spirits—whatever it be—physical miles do not count." And the devotion: "Rarest flower on earth—rarest beauty of color—rarest shape & aroma—fragrance bewildering so quieting . . . I hear a song no mortal has ever heard."

Kisses are sprinkled throughout their letters: "A kiss.—Two.—Three . . . Another kiss.—I'll eat a sandwich . . . Another kiss . . . Still another gentle kiss"; "All my love goes to you—And the kiss that is my life," and almost every letter ends with a kiss, at least one ("An endless kiss till you struggle for some air"; "a kiss goodnight—a real one"; "A tiny kiss"; and "I kiss you—any way you wish—but I prefer that it be lively"), and often more than one: "Loads and loads of kisses—All kinds."

"You in the lake—You in the trees—You in the smell of the soil—You in the windstorm—You in the most vivid lightning—You too in the crashes of thunder—You in the marvelous colors of day-break—You everywhere—Every moment—Giving me strength—Great—Great quick strength," wrote Stieglitz.

"I thought of you—but I've thought of you all along Dearest," promised O'Keeffe. Thoughts, love, kisses survive, even *thrive,* in the letters left behind.

In 1998, a burial ground in South Korea was excavated to make way for new housing. During excavation of the tombs, a burial chamber was unearthed and a letter that had been placed with the occupant came to light. It was over four hundred years old, written by a wife to her dead husband.

"You used to tell me that we would live together until our hairs turned gray and we would die together . . . How come you forget that and go away first and leave me behind? Take me with you now because I cannot live after losing you and I want to follow your way. I cannot let go of my heart toward you in this world and my grief is endless . . . I write only briefly but cannot continue any longer for my heart is so torn apart."

It was a common practice in Korea at the time to bury family letters with the body of the deceased; in this tomb there were seventeen other letters written to the dead man. But it is the wife's letter that brims with the painful fervor of longing; she seems to be with us, tugging on our sleeves for an answer to her question: *Why did he leave me?*

"Read this carefully, come to me in my dreams, and tell me all," she begs in the final lines of the letter. "I believe I will see you in my dreams."

James Joyce met Nora Barnacle in June 1904 in Dublin. Their first date was on June 16, when they took a walk down by the banks of the Liffey. Lounging against the river wall, Nora reached down into Joyce's pants and, as Joyce would describe it years later, "frigged me slowly." June 16 is celebrated around the world as Bloomsday, a celebration of a day in the life of Leopold Bloom, as presented in Joyce's novel *Ulysses*. But not everyone knows about the inspiration behind the date or what it commemorates.

A courtship of sorts followed that first date, with letters to fill in the times the two were apart. "Your glove lay beside me all night—unbuttoned—but other wise conducted itself very properly," Joyce wrote to Nora in July, and weeks later: "I have been sitting in an easy chair like a fool. I could do nothing. I could hear nothing but your voice. I am like a fool hearing you call me 'Dear.' I offended two men today by leaving them coolly. I wanted to hear your voice, not theirs."

In September he wrote, "When I am happy I have an insane wish to tell it to everyone I meet but I would be much happier if you gave me one of those chirruping kisses you are fond of giving me. They remind me of canaries singing."

Just four months after they met, Joyce convinced Nora to leave Ireland with him. Together they set out for the Continent, where they would live an itinerant life for twenty-eight years, settling in various cities around Europe. Joyce's love letters to Nora continued through the decades, written when they were living together ("Nothing you can do will annoy me tonight . . . I will kiss you a hundred times") and when they had to be apart: "Guide me, my saint, my angel . . . O, take me in to your soul of souls and then I will indeed become the poet of my race . . . My body will soon penetrate into yours, O that my soul could enter too! . . . O how I long to feel your body mingled with mine, to see you faint and faint and faint under my kiss!"

My favorite Joyce love letter is one he wrote in apology—"What a worthless fellow I am!"—after accusing Nora (wrongly) of cheating on him. "Do you know what a pearl is and what an opal is?" he asked her in the letter. "My soul when you came sauntering to me first through those sweet summer evenings was beautiful but with the pale passionless beauty of a pearl. Your love has passed through me and now I feel my mind something like an opal, that is, full of strange uncertain hues and colors, of warm lights and quick shadows and of broken music."

Joyce also wrote lusty letters to Nora: "Side by side and inside this spiritual love I have for you there is also a wild beast-like craving for every inch of your body, for every secret and shameful part of it, for every odour and act of it." Those letters are ripe with pornographic proposals and festooned with lurid details of "blocking" (intercourse), "frigging" (masturbation), and "dirty fat girlish farts" (no translation needed).

In reading those, I appreciate even more the veil of privacy afforded by letters, since I wish this time I had *not* been the fly on the wall observing Joyce's sexual adventures. But I do like having a peek at his love: "A million kisses to my darling dew-laden western flower, a million million kisses to my dear Nora of the curls."

For eighteen years of his life Nelson Mandela was imprisoned on Robben Island, off the coast of Cape Town in South Africa. He was confined to a small cell, allowed few visitors, and had only rare opportunities to post letters. He used those opportunities to write to his wife, Winnie.

"Your beautiful photo still stands about two feet above my left shoulder as I write this note," he wrote to her in 1976, twelve years into his imprisonment on Robben Island. "I dust it carefully every morning, for to do so gives me the pleasant feeling that I'm caressing you as in the old days. I even touch your nose with mine to recapture the electric current that used to flush through my blood whenever I did so."

For Mandela, the letters he wrote to his wife brought him sustenance and satisfaction: "Whenever I write you, I feel that inside physical warmth, that makes me forget all my problems. I become full of love."

Letters as tokens, talismans, reminders: we can leave behind the best of what we have been, what we have given. Love. And how wonderful it is that in letters we can be so free in loving. When I write a love letter, I allow myself the privacy to say exactly what I mean, and I say it with singularity—I write my love letters for one very specific and beloved person. When I get such letters in return, I am reminded of how love is shared.

Daniel Kahneman, Nobel Prize–winning psychologist, noted the phenomenon of what I call negative recollection: we tend to remember the bad things said to us and about us, rather than the good things. His advice for married couples is that it might be more important to ease back on criticism rather than crank up the praise. But how about writing a letter telling your spouse how much you love him or her? Whenever he or she needed reassurance, the letter would be there, ready to read over and over again. No memory required, for the moment is saved forever in a letter. I turn to Jack's letters when I am feeling a bit lost—and I find what makes me whole, all over again.

After his younger brother, Eddie, died at age twenty-five, my husband wrote to me, "I don't wish anymore. Sometimes I dream though . . . I hold my infant son and hug my almost grown daughter, I thirst for life, for love, for meaning . . . when I touch my Nina I ask no questions at all—being is enough." For both of us, to be together, in love, has been enough.

My mother signs her letters to me with love ("I love you and your groom-to-be and your pussycat! Kisses to all," she wrote, just before my wedding). She writes to me with news, maybe a bit of advice, and always affection. I remember getting a letter from her in which she'd copied a quote from the French philosopher Hélène Cixous: "If, in a warm night a woman touches an apple with a knowing, loving hand, then, in a cold night another woman feels that hand holding an apple, and that hand keeps her from surrendering to despair."

Below the quotation my mother wrote in words that still feed my soul today: "Let's always hand each other apples, even when we're far apart." We have handed each other comfort, back and forth over the decades, letters being our apples (like for Carson and Freeman). We save our letters to be reread, the fruit full of sustenance and flavor.

Charles Adams, father of the photographer Ansel Adams, wrote to his son when Ansel's first child was born in 1933. Drawing upon his own experiences as a father, he explained, "This boy of yours will reach down into the depths of your hearts and touch the strings there, to sound such rich chords . . . [that] will fill your being with a joy unknown before and a happiness, which we cannot define, through many, many years." I know such love, and letters I've written are witness to it. Louisa May Alcott, famous for *Little Women* and scores of other books, essays, and short stories, became the stand-in mother for her niece Lulu when her sister May died just weeks after giving birth. Louisa was devastated by the death; she had loved her sister May intensely and based the character Amy from *Little Women* on her. May left her daughter, Lulu, to be raised by Louisa, and despite her heavy workload and existing family responsibilities (including caring for her aging father, Bronson Alcott), Louisa was eager to take on the care of the baby. As she wrote to a friend in 1880, "Little Lu is a very remarkable child . . . I fancy I shall feel as full of responsibility as a hen with one chick, & cluck and scratch industriously for the sole benefit of my daughter." A year later, she wrote of Lulu as "the sweet baby who is an unspeakable comfort."

When Lulu was old enough to receive letters of her own, Alcott wrote to her with love and kisses: "I long to grab my tall girl & feel her arms around me, & her rosy cheek on mine . . .

XXXXXX" and "Six little dogs are tumbling & playing in the snow opposite. If my blue girl was there I'd like it better. Love to all and XXX kisses to Lulu." When she was hospitalized for chronic health problems, Louisa wrote to her Lulu, "Just now a great barge with six horses came up to the hotel full of children . . . I wish I saw a little curly girl in a blue dress and hat among them. I should fly out & grab her & give her *hundreds* of kisses."

Before she died in 1888, Alcott completed her book titled *Lulu's Library*, offering as an introduction, "These stories were told to my little niece in our quiet hour before bedtime." The collection of stories is a pretty tribute to the little girl she adored, but it is in her letters to Lulu and about Lulu that I find, forever alive, the love of an aunt for her adopted daughter: "Her picture hangs over my table, & another one of her at the foot of the bed, so I see her all the time & think about her a great deal . . . I love to think of her so well and happy."

The poet Anne Sexton wrote letters to her daughters when they were away from her at camp, college, or boarding school. The youngest daughter, Joy, was sent to boarding school when Sexton left her husband, Kayo; both the pending divorce and her forced separation made the girl miserable. Sexton tried to console her daughter by letter: "My love is with you like a pillow (if and when you need or reach out for it) always, always, always."

It wasn't the first time Joy had been separated from her mother. Her birth had sent Sexton into a prolonged bout of depression and for the first two years of her life, the child lived with her paternal grandparents while her older sister, Linda, was sent around to live with various relatives. The pattern would be repeated again and again during the years of the girls' childhood, when Sexton was hospitalized for mental illness and the girls were farmed out to others.

The letters Sexton wrote to her daughters during these times sought to reassure them of her abiding love, despite the constraints and burdens of her mental illness: "I would tear down a star and put it into a smart jewelry box if I could," she wrote to Linda. "I would seal up the love in a long thin bottle so that you could sip it whenever it was needed."

In 1969, Sexton wrote a letter to Linda, when Linda was sixteen and Sexton was forty. She wrote it while on a flight to St. Louis, after reading a story in the *New Yorker* that reminded her of her own mother, with whom she had had a difficult relationship, "And I thought of you—someday flying somewhere all alone and me dead perhaps and you wishing to speak to me. And I want to speak back . . . This is my message to the forty-year-old Linda.

"Life is not easy. It is awfully lonely. I know that. Now you too know it—wherever you are . . . I love you, 40-year-old Linda, and I love what you do, what you find, what you are! . . . Talk to my poems, and talk to your heart—I'm in both: if you need me."

Sexton committed suicide in 1974, at the age of forty-five. Twenty years later, Linda published a book about her relationship with her mother, a tangle of pain and abuse and abandonment. And yet through it all, the letters were saved: "A letter from my mother was always precious—her natural abundance well suited to the expressive nature of letter writing—and I had saved nearly every one I had ever received."

For it is in the letters that Sexton spoke most clearly to her daughters: "I love you. You are closest to my heart, closer than any other human being. You are my extension. You are my prayer. You are my belief in God. For better or worse, you inherit me."

In 1875, a woman left her infant child on the steps of the New York Foundling Hospital. Pinned to the bundle was a letter. "Alone and deserted, I need to put my little one with you for a time. I would willingly work and take care of her but no one will have me and her too . . . She is only three weeks old . . . No one knows how awful it is to separate from their child but a mother, but,

I trust you will be kind and the only consolation I have is if . . . I lead an honest life that the Father of us all will permit us to be united."

Thousands of children were abandoned by their hopeless parents in the late 1800s, left on street corners or on the steps of hospitals or orphan asylums. Jobs were scarce, food expensive, housing hard to find and keep. Leaving children to the care of someone else seemed the only way to keep the children alive.

"Will you let some good nurse take charge of him and will you try to find some kind hearted lady to adopt him and love him as her own while he is young that he may never know but what she is his own mother? It would break my heart to have him grow up without a mother to love and care for him. God only knows the bitter anguish of my heart in parting with this little dear, still if it costs me my life I am obliged to give him up." Letters like these, numbering in the hundreds, fill the archives of the state institutions that took over the care of children left behind by their parents.

Mary Van Allen left her infant son Robbie at the Albany Orphan Asylum in New York in 1884. Desperate and miserable as she was, she was still hopeful that she would be able to return one day and retrieve the beloved boy: "Will you please to watch Robbie A little . . . now please don't have him forget that hes got A mother . . . i hope and pray that he will grown up to be a Christian and love his mother. May god love and protect him All of his life . . . tell Robbie that ma ma wants to see him and kiss him for me & god bless you to take care of my little boy."

Through the ensuing years, Van Allen wrote to the orphanage often, inquiring after Robbie and receiving letters back from the administrators, news about his health and his learning. In one letter, a kind administrator added at the end, "He sends ever so much love to you."

I don't know whether the letters Mary wrote to the asylum were kept for her son, as proof for that little boy that somewhere out there his mother loved him. But I do know that twenty-five years later, Mary Van Allen and her son Robbie were reunited: "I have found her at last," Robbie wrote in a letter back to the orphanage where he'd spent his childhood, "and I am living with her."

Just weeks before his death in May 1895, the Cuban nationalist José Martí sent a letter to his mother, explaining his commitment to Cuban independence and freedom from Spain. Martí had been fighting the battle since he was sixteen years old, when he was first imprisoned for fomenting revolution. From prison he wrote one of his first letters to his mother: "I am very sorry to be behind bars, but my imprisonment is very useful to me. It has given me plenty of lessons for my life."

In his last letter to his mother, he wrote, "I think

of you ceaselessly . . . you are pained by the sacrifice of my life—but then why was I born from you with a life that loves sacrifice? . . . The duty of a man lies where he is most useful. But in my growing and necessary agony the memory of my mother is with me always . . . Now give me your blessing and believe that no work that is not charitable and pure will ever emerge from my heart."

In the postscript to the letter he added, "Truth and tenderness are not useless. Do not suffer."

Love. How to be remembered, and how to remember. Love remains, vital and strong, in the letters I leave behind.

12

Taking Flight

> to live and write like one of the first; to be
> free and general and not at all afraid; to
> feel, understand, and express everything.
> —Henry James, *The Aspern Papers*

We live in a postpostal age. Digital messages
have largely replaced written communications. I still get deliveries to my street-side
mailbox, mostly thank-you cards and birthday and
holiday greetings (along with bills, political pleas,
and catalogs of all kinds). My mother still writes
to me, and a few friends take the time to scrawl
out their thoughts, stuff them in an envelope, affix
a stamp, and send their message across miles or
blocks or continents. Yet many of these same
correspondents also communicate to me, and I
back to them, through e-mails and texts, Twitter
and Facebook.

Digital messaging allows communication without contact. It is easy and fast, and for the most
part dependable. I cannot imagine living without
e-mail, going back to the stone age of phone

calls and phone tag to set up meetings or make plans. Facebook keeps me in the loop of so many friends' lives and events, and nothing is faster than Twitter for expressing an opinion.

Why do I write letters? I have looked back over millennia of letter writing to understand, and I have found so many reasons to write a letter: to build a bridge across time and space, to write in privacy, to find proof, to create a unique and singular document. I have discovered in letters tenderness and kindness, advice and immortality, and I have been witness to love, all kinds and forms and sorts of love.

V. S. Naipaul and his father wrote back and forth to each other when Vidia went off to Oxford in 1950 on scholarship, leaving the island of Trinidad and the Naipaul clan behind. The letters from father to son contain the expected fatherly counsel: "So long as you use your freedom and feeling of independence sensibly all will be good" and the often repeated "Keep your centre." I especially love the advice Dad offered, that there is "no harm in kissing a girl, so long as you do not become too prone for that sort of thing."

The letters written by Naipaul senior to his son contain more than just advice and concern. The letters are a shared conversation between two men, one young (just seventeen) and the other well into middle age. Father and son were similar in ways that no one in their circle of family and friends in Trinidad could ever entirely understand. Both were writers ("Long years ago, when I was 14 or 16, I felt much as you are feeling now; eager to write"), and both were sensitive to the personalities and situations that make the world interesting, as well as the difficulties in re-creating that world through writing. As Naipaul senior wrote to Vidia, "We must learn to look at people objectively. Per-ception is rare and intelligence is by no means widespread. Those who have it to any unusual degree often suffer terribly; they are the most lonesome creatures in the world."

Naipaul senior used his weekly letters to his son to continue their long discussions of ideas and concepts ("What do you think literature boils down to?") and to extend the kinship between them: "I so long to write," he wrote. "This is the time for me to be myself. When shall I get the chance? I don't know. I come from work, dead tired. The *Guardian* [the newspaper where he worked] is taking all out of me—writing tosh. What price salted fish and things of that sort. Actually that is my assignment for tomorrow! It hurts."

Vidia answered his father with letters that encouraged him to keep writing—"If I were you, I should send interesting bits of news to the *News Chronicle* [British daily paper] . . . It is not too late"—and with thanks for the letters from home: "What a delight to receive Pa's excellent letter from home. If I didn't know the man, I would have said: what a delightful father to have."

"DO NOT SAY YOU RESIGN YOURSELF TO OBSCURITY," Naipaul senior instructed his son, following up with the encouraging words "Or if you do, say that in obscurity you will do your work. Let it be a shield to you from the noise and inanities of the rest."

Vidia responded with thanks, and with encouragement of his own, which his father joyfully adopted: "You say I should write at least 500 words every day," he wrote to his son. "Well, I have started to do so, but cannot say much just now. Let me first see how well the resolve works out."

When Vidia's confidence sagged, his father was there to offer consolation: "That rejection [of a manuscript] gave you, as it would have given me, a nasty jolt. But people such as you do not remain submerged for long. People like us are like corks thrown on water: we may go down momentarily; but we simply must pop up again."

"When your university studies are over, if you do get a good job, all well and good; if you do not, you have not got to worry one little bit," Naipaul senior wrote to junior. "You will come home—and do what I am longing to do now: just write; and read and do the things you like to do. This is where I may be of some use to you. I want you to have that chance which I have never had: somebody to support me and mine while I write . . . Remember, you haven't got to worry after you are through with Oxford. Your work is cut out. I stand back of you."

Vidia wrote to his father, "You, only on the right side of fifty, can still consider yourself in the prime of life . . . You can come to live with me." He was just finishing up at Oxford and planned on staying in England, having found an English-woman he longed to marry (Patricia Hale) and hoping to find a job.

Naipaul senior was thrilled: "The others have begun calling me 'Englishman,' because you say I am to come and live with you."

But two months later, V. S. Naipaul's father died. Stricken, Vidia wrote to his mother: "I have to abandon the idea of growing older in Pa's company; and I have to get the strength to stand alone."

V. S. Naipaul would come to understand that in fact his father *was* always there beside him; there was no need to stand alone. His father was there in memories and in photos, and in the books that the son would write, including his first novel, *A House for Mr. Biswas*, inspired by the life of his father. And his father was with him in the letters they exchanged and that Naipaul had saved. Those letters brought father and son together during those first university years, and then later, again and again, whenever Naipaul reread them.

Sitting in my kitchen, I finish rereading the letters of Naipaul, father and son, contained now in a published volume. I look over to the kitchen table where I've left my box of stationery, one piece of cream-white paper pulled out. Beside the box sits my tarnished silver teabag bowl where I keep my Forever stamps, and the pen I use to write my weekly letters to Peter.

When I write a letter I begin the equation, I open the circle, I take a step toward connection. Writing a letter is a kind of redemption mixed in with creation mixed in with faith, absolute faith that what I write will travel across miles and bring me close to the one I write to.

V. S. Naipaul's father crossed an ocean to stand beside his son, through his letters. Letters that kept him present and vibrant in his son's life, years beyond the first writing.

When I sit down to write to Peter, I am placing myself beside him and drawing a space around us. He becomes the focus. I am as absorbed with him as I was when he was a baby lying so sweetly on my bed, or a six-year-old, just home from school with something new to show me, or a sixteen-year-old, driving with his learner's permit and me beside him, white-knuckled and mute with fear. I paid him attention then and I pay him attention now.

I write my letters without caution or constraint. I am a mother who worries and brags, shares and listens. I listen. In telling stories and asking questions, I am listening. And I can hear Peter's voice in my head as I write on. I start a circle and invite its completion. And in that half-finished circle Peter and I are together. If he writes me back, the circle is complete. But even if he doesn't write back to me, the arc is there, the shape of a mother's arm curved around her child.

Why write a letter?

In the arena where so much can go wrong—the place where parents and children meet and circle and pause—letters offer us another chance. Distance is reversed, connection made possible again. The qualities of a good letter are also the qualities of a good relationship. Letters are the tangible manifestation of the trust I put in my child, the singularity of our kinship, the importance of our shared experiences, and the care and effort that is taken in our conversations. Letters are the physical tokens of kindness we show each other, and are the proof of my allegiance and our alliance. Letters are abiding and durable. Letters are markers of our love.

There is no pressure of time or deadlines or immediacy in the letters between Peter and me: there is the give-and-take of extending, waiting, receiving. Wisdom offered, or simply advice born of experience (which is the greatest wisdom). There is love, underlying it all, promised and granted and lasting. And there is flight, flight not away from someone but toward everything that matters.

Up in my closet, I've stored the bins containing the letters of James Seligman in stacked rows, two up, two across. I go up there from time to time to sit on the floor and read a letter or two (or three). I like to feel the paper in my hand, touch where James touched, using his pen to share all the news with his mother. I know she wrote him back because he mentions her notes, answers her questions, thanks her for the checks. It doesn't matter that I don't have any of his mother's letters, because the letters I do have are enough.

A son's arm encircling his mother's waist, the love shared between two.

Acknowledgments

. . . I cannot but wonder at the diligence of those gentlemen—the postilions—who spend their lives galloping back and forth to carry our mail. There is not a day in the week, not an hour in the day when they are not on the road! Those wonderful fellows! What a marvelous invention is the postal service! . . . I am sometimes tempted to write to thank them, and I think I would have done so, had the thought not occurred to me that . . . perhaps they are tempted to write to thank me for writing the letters which they are paid to deliver.

—Madame de Sévigné

Thank you to the postal workers who have carried mail for centuries. My heart warms at the sight of letters in my box and I am grateful for the men and women who carry them to me.

Many friends have shared their letters with me. I want to give special thanks to Viveca Van Bladel, Amy Schneider, Debra Rapka Zyla, Bev and Charles Stanley, Thomas, 8th Lord Stanley of

Alderley, Nancy Shulins, Catherine Jacobi, Stephanie Young, Betsy and John Young, Roger Angell, and Nancy Brett. Friends also have shared stories about letters, and I thank Lauren Pair, Marta Smith Campbell, Ellison Garvin Weist, Sharon Mooradian, Louella Smith-Rabsatt, Jenee Day, and Jennifer. I have had many wonderful conversations about letters with many people at dinner parties, library meetings, and walks along the beach, and I thank you all.

I am grateful to Stuart Emmrich and Dorothy Ko for their interest and help, and to my friend Tazewell Thompson for being a constant source of inspiration. Gary Dean Timm writes prolific and totemic letters, and I am lucky to be one of his correspondents. Bev Stanley took care of me through heat waves, power outages, and fevers, and I thank her.

I am thankful for the help of the kind staff of the Connecticut Historical Society in Hartford and of the Schomburg Center for Research in Black Culture, of the New York Public Library, and I am always grateful to and for the librarians of the Westport Public Library.

Thank you to the marvelous Esther Newberg, who shares my reverence for letters and to whom I owe bucketloads of thank-you cards for all that she does for me.

Thank you to Alice Mayhew and Karyn Marcus, without whom I could not have brought my love of letters to print. It has been an honor and a pleasure working with both of you. Thank you also to Jonathan Cox for all his help and patience and to Laura Wise. Thank you to Elisa Rivlin for her wise counsel.

I send through the mail and through this book my everlasting thank-yous to my husband, Jack, who writes the letters that steal my heart and seal the deal over and over again; to my sister, Natasha, and my parents, Tilde and Tola, who have written to me and loved me all my life and whose letters I cherish; to my mother-in-law, Patricia Menz, who writes with grace and care and love; and to my children, Peter, Michael, George, Martin, and Meredith, whose cards and notes fill my green trunk to the top.

Grateful acknowledgment is made to the following for translations and excerpts used herein: *Epistolary Korea: Letters in the Communicative Space of the Choson, 1392–1910*, edited by Jahyun Kim Haboush; *Letters from Ancient Egypt*, translated by Edward F. Wente and edited by Edmund S. Meltzer; *The Letters of Abelard and Heloise*, translated by Betty Radice; and *Segues: A Correspondence in Poetry*, by William Stafford and Marvin Bell.

In addition, I would like to thank David Royko; Marvin Bell; Razia Saleh and the Nelson Mandela Foundation; Linda Gray Sexton; and the heirs of James Seligman for their kind permissions and support.

Bibliography

I am tired, Beloved, of chafing my heart
    against
The want of you;
Of squeezing it into little inkdrops,
And posting it.
        —Amy Lowell, *"The Letter"*

For more information, and great reading pleasure, I recommend the following:

Always, Rachel: The Letters of Rachel Carson and Dorothy Freeman, 1952–1964. Edited by Martha Freeman. Boston: Beacon Press, 1995.

Anne Sexton: A Self-Portrait in Letters. Edited by Linda Gray Sexton and Lois Ames. Boston: Houghton Mifflin, 1977.

Beloved Sisters and Loving Friends: Letters from Rebecca Primus of Royal Oak, Maryland, and Addie Brown of Hartford, Connecticut, 1854–1868. Edited by Farah Jasmine Griffin. New York: Knopf, 1999.

Between Father and Son: Family Letters. V. S.

Naipaul. Edited by Gillon Aitken. New York: Knopf, 2000.

Blacks in Bondage: Letters of American Slaves. Edited by Robert S. Starobin. New York: Barnes & Noble Books, 1998.

"Cicero's Letters and Roman Epistolary Etiquette." Jenny D. Drucknemiller. A thesis presented to the Department of Classics and the Graduate School of the University of Oregon, December 2007.

Days of Grace. Arthur Ashe and Arnold Rampersad. New York: Ballantine Books, 1993.

Dear Jay, Love Dad: Bud Wilkinson's Letters to His Son. Jay Wilkinson. Norman: University of Oklahoma Press, 2012.

Dear Sammy: Letters from Gertrude Stein and Alice B. Toklas. Edited with a memoir by Samuel M. Steward. Boston: Houghton Mifflin, 1977.

Dear Sister: Medieval Women and the Epistolary Genre. Edited by Karen Cherewatuk and Ulrike Wiethaus. Philadelphia: University of Pennsylvania Press, 1993.

Epistolary Korea: Letters in the Communicative Space of the Chŏson, 1392–1910. Edited by Jahyun Kim Haboush. New York: Columbia University Press, 2009.

Epistolary Practices: Letter Writing in America before Telecommunications. William Merrill

Decker. Chapel Hill: University of North Carolina Press, 1998.

"The Female World of Love and Ritual: Relations between Women in Nineteenth-Century America." Caroll Smith-Rosenberg. *Signs* 1, no. 1 (Autumn 1975): 1–29.

Floating Worlds: The Letters of Edward Gorey & Peter F. Neumeyer. Edited by Peter F. Neumeyer. San Francisco: Pomegranate Communications, 2011.

The Flowers of Friendship: Letters Written to Gertrude Stein. Edited by Donald Gallup. New York: Knopf, 1953.

F. Scott Fitzgerald: Letters to His Daughter. Edited by Andrew Turnbull. New York: Charles Scribner's Sons, 1963.

Gender, Society, and Print Culture in Late Stuart England: The Cultural World of the Athenian Mercury. Helen Berry. Burlington, VT: Ashgate, 2003.

The Gentlest Art. Edited by E. V. Lucas. London: Methuen & Co., 1907.

Gertrude and Alice. Diana Souhami. London: Pandora Press, 1991.

"Goat on a Cow." *Radiolab*, September 10, 2007. http://www.radiolab.org/2007/sep/10/goat-on-a-cow/.

Heloise and Abelard: A New Biography. James Burge. San Francisco: HarperSanFrancisco, 2003.

H. H. Asquith: Letters to Venetia Stanley. Selected and edited by Michael and Eleanor Brock. New York: Oxford University Press, 1982.

I Remember Arthur Ashe: Memories of a True Tennis Pioneer and Champion of Social Causes by the People Who Knew Him. Compiled by Mike Towle. Nashville: Cumberland House, 2001.

Letters from Ancient Egypt. Translated by Edward F. Wente and edited by Edmund S. Meltzer. Atlanta: Scholars Press, 1990.

Letters left with orphans in the nineteenth century: http://www.orphantraindepot.com/NYFH Letters.html.

The Letters of Abelard and Heloise. Translated by Betty Radice. New York: Penguin Books, 1974.

Letters of a Nation: A Collection of Extraordinary American Letters. Edited by Andrew Carroll. New York: Kodansha International, 1997.

The Letters of Edith Wharton. Edited by R. W. B. Lewis and Nancy Lewis. New York: Collier Books, 1988.

The Letters of Emily Dickinson. Edited by Mabel Loomis Todd. New York: Dover, 2003.

The Letters of Gertrude Stein and Thornton Wilder. Edited by Edward M. Burns, Ulla E. Dydo, and William Rice. New Haven, CT: Yale University Press, 1996.

The Letters of Mary Wollstonecraft Shelley. Edited

by Betty T. Bennett. Baltimore: Johns Hopkins University Press, 1980.

Letters of slaves: http://library.duke.edu/ruben stein/collections/digitized/african-american-women/.

"Letter Writing in America." Kathryn Burke. National Postal Museum. http://www.postal museum.si.edu/letterwriting/lw06.html.

Lord Chesterfield's Letters. Edited by David Roberts. New York: Oxford University Press, 1992.

The Love Letters of Abelard and Heloise. Israel Gollancz. R. M. Dent. 1908. Reprint, Charleston, SC: Forgotten Books, 2007.

Madame de Sévigné: A Life and Letters. Frances Mossiker. New York: Knopf, 1983.

A Memoir of Friendship: The Letters Between Carol Shields and Blanche Howard. Edited by Blanche Howard and Allison Howard. Toronto, ON: Viking Canada, 2007.

M. F. K. Fisher: A Life in Letters. Edited by Norah K. Barr, Marsha Moran and Patrick Moran. Berkeley, CA: Counterpoint, 1997.

The Murder of Helen Jewett. Patricia Cline Cohen. New York: Vintage, 1999.

My Faraway One: Selected Letters of Georgia O'Keeffe and Alfred Stieglitz. Edited by Sarah Greenough. New Haven, CT: Yale University Press, 2011.

Our Crowd: The Great Jewish Families of New

York. Stephen Birmingham. Syracuse, NY: Syracuse University Press, 1967.

The Oxford Book of Letters. Edited by Frank Kermode and Anita Kermode. New York: Oxford University Press, 1995.

"A Point of View: Mourning the Loss of the Written Word." BBC News Magazine, February 3, 2012. http://www.bbc.co.uk/news/magazine-16871715.

The Postal Age: The Emergence of Modern Communications in Nineteenth-Century America. David M. Henkin. Chicago: University of Chicago Press, 2006.

Royko in Love: Mike's Letters to Carol. Edited by David Royko. Chicago: University of Chicago Press, 2010.

Searching for Mercy Street: My Journey Back to My Mother. Linda Gray Sexton. Boston: Little, Brown, 1994.

The Second Post. Edited by E. V. Lucas. London: Methuen & Co., 1910.

Secret Historian: The Life and Times of Samuel Steward, Professor, Tattoo Artist, and Sexual Renegade. Justin Spring. New York: Farrar, Straus and Giroux, 2010.

Segues: A Correspondence in Poetry. William Stafford and Marvin Bell. Boston: David R. Godine, 1983.

Selected Letters of James Joyce. Edited by Richard Ellmann. New York: Viking Press, 1975.

The Selected Letters of Louisa May Alcott. Edited by Joel Myerson, Daniel Shealy, and Madeleine B. Stern. Boston: Little, Brown, 1987.

"Silence, Exile, Punning: James Joyce's Chance Encounters." Louis Menand. *New Yorker*, July 2, 2012.

The Stanleys of Alderley: Their Letters Between the Years 1851–1865. Edited by Nancy Mitford. Norwich, UK: Whitefriars Press, 1939.

Staying On Alone: Letters of Alice B. Toklas. Edited by Edward Burns. New York: Liveright, 1973.

Women on the Margins: Three Seventeenth Century Lives. Natalie Zemon Davis. Cambridge, MA: Harvard University Press, 1995.

Women's Letters: America from the Revolutionary War to the Present. Edited by Lisa Grunwald and Stephen J. Adler. New York: Dial Press, 2005.

Word from New France: The Selected Letters of Marie de L'Incarnation. Marie de L'Incarnation. Translated by Joyce Marshall. Toronto, ON: Oxford University Press, 1967.

Center Point Large Print
600 Brooks Road / PO Box 1
Thorndike ME 04986-0001 USA

(207) 568-3717

US & Canada:
1 800 929-9108
www.centerpointlargeprint.com